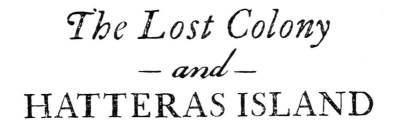

The Lost Colony
— and —
HATTERAS ISLAND

D0113108

The Lost Colony
— and —
HATTERAS ISLAND

Scott Dawson

THE
History
PRESS

Published by The History Press
Charleston, SC
www.historypress.com

Copyright © 2020 by Scott Dawson
All rights reserved

Front cover, bottom, and back cover: Library of Congress.

First published 2020

Manufactured in the United States

ISBN 9781467144339

Library of Congress Control Number: 2020930467

Sands of Time

Buried by the sands of time,
Blown in by the burning winds,
Like lost whispers of the pine,
A story lurks within.
A shattered civilization that no longer makes a sound,
Gone but not forgotten as we sink spades into the ground.
We honor those who came before and lent a helping hand,
No longer will you be ignored and sit beneath the sand.

—original poem by Scott Davis Dawson

CONTENTS

CONTENTS

FOREWORD

I first met Scott late one evening having driven from the Norfolk airport, where I had arrived that day from the UK. He was alone, looking after his father's motel in Buxton. There in the corner of the reception was a heap of artifacts that he had gathered up over the years across Hatteras Island, as holiday homes were being built on the ancient sites. "Could this brick be Tudor?" was the first exchange we had in the eerie reception of that motel. But I had come over as a historical archaeologist, excavating Elizabethan sites in England and intrigued by the saga of the Lost Colony, thinking it might be a simple tale for an Englishman to resolve. Ten years later, and a whole mountain of excavation all over Hatteras Island, I now think we are closer to solving the mystery than ever, and this book tells the story.

Scott is born and bred a Hatterasman from a family tree that reliably goes back to the eighteenth century. He is related to most of the original families on the island and is a passionate advocate for its history and heritage. But Hatteras Island is remote and can only be reached by ferry or a long car journey along forty miles of finger-wide sand dune that gets washed by every passing hurricane. The consequence is that it has been all too often forgotten by historians, happier to reside in their metropolitan libraries than this outpost of America. Scott's passion and diligence stemmed from a frustration that what was clearly documented as the first foothold of the English in the New World was being denied by these historians. How could they avoid the conclusion that when John White returned to Roanoke in 1590 to find the inscription "CRO" on the oak tree or, even more clearly, "CROATOAN" on the fort's palisade they had evacuated there, to the safety of the island of their Indian ally Manteo?

The answer, Scott believes, is that there are too many big dollars to be made out of the Lost Colony story and that to have a mystery is far better for the box office than a solution. But this is not science; this is where archaeology comes in. From that first meeting with Scott, we have been working together to find that crucial archaeological evidence to show that the abandoned colonists survived on Hatteras Island from around 1587, making their lives first as a colony but, having given up hope that they would be rescued, soon moving into the Indian villages, forming relationships, spawning children and creating families. Their descendants, the Hatteras Indians, were able to forge a successful life on the island, surviving until at least 1700 as the "blue-eyed Indians" observed by John Lawson, the next Englishman to record the Outer Banks, since the writings of Thomas Harriot 120 years earlier.

This book has emerged out of this collaboration between our archaeological research and Scott's sensitive reevaluation of historical and ethnographic sources. Every spring, I have brought a group of archaeology students to Hatteras, where, with the help of the volunteers of the Croatoan Archaeological Society, we have been discreetly investigating many of the potential sites where the colonists might have engaged with the Native American communities. What has emerged is a complex story of interaction; there is not a "smoking gun" piece of evidence, a single item that proves that they came here in 1587, but a compelling narrative that extends into the seventeenth century that tells of a singular society, spanning the two worlds that hunted with firearms, wore European dress, worked copper and traded with the English farther up the coast in Jamestown. This could only have been through the entanglement of English and American culture.

In today's world, with the emergence of nationalist politics, popularism and the miscasting of the past to serve the present, the Lost Colony story continues to have resonance today among certain political activists and writers. It is therefore important that a more unbiased and scientifically based account is presented to show that the first English to have settled in North America survived among Native Americans and that their descendants may still be living, unidentified, today.

FOREWORD

I commend Scott's book to you; it is very much his personal journey of discovery and one that is written by someone who knows every inch of the landscape and every part of its history. It is not a formal scientific report of our many discoveries together—this will have to wait a little longer for the many careful analyses to be completed—but I hope this will serve as a taster for what might be coming in the future.

—Professor Mark Horton
Professor of Archaeology and Culture History
Royal Agricultural University
Cirencester
England

PREFACE

Growing up on the Outer Banks, I was familiar with the Lost Colony mystery. As a child, I had seen the *Lost Colony* play and heard the mythology of 114 English colonists who vanished on Roanoke Island, leaving only one clue as to their whereabouts: the word *Croatoan* carved on a tree. It was not until I was an adult and finished with college that I discovered the real history surrounding the colony that eventually led to digging them up. It started with simply reading the primary sources and collecting Indian pottery from construction sites and evolved into a multinational archaeological dig that has now appeared on the History Channel, Discovery Channel, Travel Channel and *National Geographic* magazine. All credit and thanks to Dr. Mark Horton, his grad students and colleagues for traveling from the UK to North Carolina and investigating this piece of history. Also, thanks to my wife for organizing the Croatoan Archaeological Society and making these digs possible. I had no idea a team of professionals would ever come to Hatteras Island and dig up Croatoan and sixteenth-century English artifacts, but I am glad they did and am happy to have been a part of it.

The answers to where the colony disappeared to were painfully obvious and hidden in plain sight. Not once while I was in school did we learn about the English military settlements that came to the Outer Banks before the Lost Colony. I was never taught about how the Indians on the mainland were at war with the English before the colony arrived or that one of the colonists had been killed by them. I was never taught that the word *Croatoan*, left carved into a tree by the colony, was in fact Hatteras Island and that the

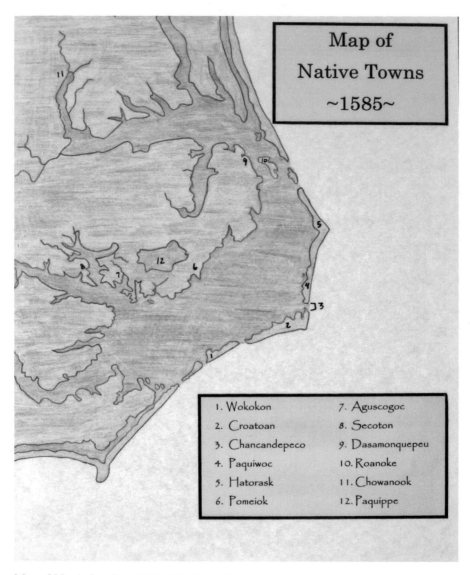

1. Wokokon   7. Aguscogoc
2. Croatoan   8. Secoton
3. Chancandepeco 9. Dasamonquepeu
4. Paquiwoc   10. Roanoke
5. Hatorask   11. Chowanook
6. Pomeiok   12. Paquippe

Map of North Carolina, 1585. *Author's collection.*

colony was very familiar with the island and the Natives there. It was not explained to me that when the governor saw the message of Croatoan he knew exactly what it meant because he had been there and lived there before and the English had a man from there (Manteo) with them in the colony.

Instead, we were fed lies in school about no one knowing what the word *Croatoan* meant, and I find this to be true with almost everyone I talk to

Hatteras Island. *Author's collection.*

about what they were told growing up. Many only learn of Plymouth Rock or Jamestown and do not know anything about voyages to North Carolina, including the myth. It is important to American history to learn about these voyages. It is the first ever contact between the English and Native Americans and the first landing of English feet on American soil.

Not only did we find sixteenth-century English artifacts in the Croatoan Indian villages but also evidence of assimilation. We now know not just where they went but also what happened after they got there. It is a story of wars, politics and adventure that ended in the coming together of two very different cultures.

INTRODUCTION

Thirty-seven years before Plymouth Rock and twenty-three years before Jamestown, the English landed in North Carolina. It was the first time the English had set foot in what is now the United States and the first time the English had any contact with Native Americans. What unfolded over the next four years is a forgotten history to most that ends with an abandoned English colony in North Carolina whose fate is largely unknown.

The legend of the Lost Colony usually goes like this: Over one hundred English colonists went to Roanoke Island in 1587 and set up a colony/ settlement. The governor of the colony, John White, went back to England for resupplies, and due to the war with Spain in Europe, he could not return for three years. When he returned, there was no trace of the colony; even the houses were gone. All that was left was a mysterious message carved on a tree that said "CROATOAN." No one has a clue what it meant. Thus, the "lost" colony.

The "lost" narrative has created the legend of the Lost Colony. It is, however, totally false. This legend was created by popular fiction. This book will show you how the colony was never lost but abandoned at Croatoan, modern-day Hatteras Island. What you will discover is the only thing that became lost was the truth.

The story of the lost colony is one of many tied together to weave a larger story of the Anglo-Spanish War. Although the war was chiefly between England and Spain, it also involved the Netherlands, Ireland and Portugal and even spilled into the Caribbean, Florida and North Carolina. The war was the number-one driving force behind the English attempts at settlement in the New World and influenced when and where they did settle. The war that brought the colony was also directly responsible for the resupply of the Lost Colony being delayed for three years and eventually the abandonment of the colony altogether.

Another story within the larger story of the Anglo-Spanish War was the very personal conflict between Queen Elizabeth of England and King Philip II of Spain, the former husband of Queen Elizabeth's older half sister Bloody Mary. England was extremely divided down religious lines, and Elizabeth constantly had to deal with internal enemies as well.

Also at this time was the often neglected story of the Croatoan Indians and their conflict with the Secotan tribe that the English would get sucked into. All of these stories shape the fate of the Lost Colony. This book will unravel the many moving parts that make up the true history of that colony. Most of what people hear about the Lost Colony is completely made up, as the story has been buried in mythology and fiction stemming from a popular play of the same name. The truth is a far more interesting story, and that is what this book is here to present.

Over twenty years of researching the primary sources surrounding the Lost Colony and over ten years of conducting archaeology on the Croatoan Indian villages have led to an understanding of what actually happened to that colony. If truth is what you seek, you will find it here.

It makes sense that such a historical place as Hatteras would yield interesting archaeology, yet until recently, this historically rich area had been virtually untapped. The full-scale archaeological excavations that are taking place each year on Hatteras Island by the Croatoan Archaeological Society (CAS) are yielding a wealth of artifacts and knowledge. Archaeologist and Professor Mark Horton from the University of Bristol (UoB), England, his team of archaeologists and the volunteers of the Croatoan Archaeological Society have been uncovering and unearthing groundbreaking, history-changing finds for the past ten years. The CAS/UoB digs have provided the most extensive archaeological research ever conducted on Hatteras Island or Croatoan, the stated destination of the "Lost" Colony.

The 1587 colony was the fourth English voyage to North Carolina. Croatoan was an island fifty miles south of Roanoke that all of the English voyages had been to and even lived on for months at a time in previous voyages. The English were very familiar with where Croatoan was and what the message on the tree meant, despite what the mythology of the Lost Colony claims. Croatoan was also the home of Manteo, an Indian the English first met in 1584 who had been to England and back twice, serving as the Lost Colony's interpreter. In addition, Governor John White told the colony that when they left Roanoke Island they should carve out the name of where they relocated to on a tree and carve a cross under the name if they left in distress.

One of the 1587 colonists, George Howe, had already been murdered by Indians from the adjacent mainland. When this murder happened, the colony actually sent twenty-five colonists to Croatoan with Manteo to get help from the Croatoan tribe. After hosting the English at a feast, the Croatoan agreed to talk to the mainland tribe called the Secotan to try to negotiate peace for the English. Instead, however, the Croatoan sacked a Secotan village/farm on the mainland and gave the corn and pumpkins that were left behind to the English. All of this happened before the governor of the colony left to get resupplies.

When Governor White returned in 1590 with resupplies, three years after he left the colonists on Roanoke, he saw the message of Croatoan and knew exactly what it meant and where the colonists had gone. He and the rest of the crew, including the captain, agreed to go to Croatoan and supply the colony. Unfortunately, a storm, coupled with near mutiny, prevented him from reconnecting with the colony. The governor, who had a daughter and granddaughter in the colony, wrote down that he was greatly joyful to find a certain token (message on the tree) of the colony being at Croatoan, the place where Manteo was born and where the people were friends of the English. Later, new explorers documenting the Hatteras tribe were told that the colony came there, and many of the Hatteras Indians had blue eyes and said their ancestors were white people who could speak out of a book and that they came on Sir Walter Raleigh's ship.

Today, archaeologists have found some of the artifacts left behind by the colony on Hatteras Island. This book is intended to set the record straight and tell the real story of what transpired on all the sixteenth-century English voyages to the New World. Once you know the facts, you will understand how completely ridiculous the Lost Colony mythology really is and always has been. More importantly, you will learn the incredible real history.

∽⬦⬦∽

FACTS FROM PRIMARY WRITTEN records, maps and documents help us to make more sense of the past, and archaeology helps fill in some of the blanks left by written records alone. The written history of the Native peoples of the entire North Carolina coastal plain region is limited to how it was seen and recorded by foreigners with unavoidable biases, because the Native peoples themselves had no form of written language. These primary written records from the initial contact period between Europeans and Native peoples are critically important in the study of Native life just prior to European influences. The primary documents and images of when Europeans first encountered the Native people of North Carolina are the only picture that historians have of how these indigenous people were living unmolested by European culture.

Since the written records about the Native people are limited to the period when contact with Europeans began, we must rely on archaeology to tell us about life in the New World long before European contact. Not only is archaeology the only way to study Native life prior to European influence, but archaeology also demonstrates the rate of assimilation between the two cultures. Archaeology gives one a look at the actual tools, weapons, diet, homes and goods people had and used at a particular time in history.

The knowledge gained about the Native Hatteras people, known as the Croatoan, and their way of life has been profound; however, the knowledge gained regarding the English-Native contact period has been astounding. What has been discovered is a story unlike any other between Europeans and Natives—a story of brotherhood and friendship rather than violence and hatred. It is a story that leads to assimilation and family, a joining of two cultures from opposite sides of the ocean and the world. It is a blending of races and culture that was a way of thinking and living far advanced for anyone of that period and even more advanced than some of the people in the world today. Men, women and children from two different worlds and cultures became one family. And while those around them were horrified at their blending of race and culture (and even still to this day there are those who wish to hide this blending of cultures and race in shame), these people were proud of their family. That is what makes this story so unique, so special. It is time we honored them for what they were and are and stop hiding them in shame. It is time to stop saying they were "lost" simply because there are those who don't want to admit they were the first assimilators, the first cross-cultural, cross-race family in America. We live in a new generation where these people no longer need to be "lost" anymore. We can proudly say they became one family because they did.

THIS BOOK IS HERE to present the finds, answer some questions and bring up some new questions as well. In archaeology, context is everything. In history, it is no different. When studying primary sources, one has to look at the historical context of the period in order to understand the perspective of the person writing down the history as they saw it/experienced it.

This book will explore both the historical context and the archaeological context in which we found the artifacts and how those contexts play a role in understanding and interpreting the finds and how those contexts paint us a picture of life on Hatteras Island through the ages. This book itself is making history in the sense that it is the first book published on any actual archaeological finds from Hatteras and the first book to place the history of Hatteras in the context of archaeology and vice versa.

— *Part I* —
THE HISTORY

Chapter 1

THE PUSH FOR COLONIZATION

A lthough the English were late in the game in their attempts at colonizing America (French, Spanish and most of western Europe had already attempted), it was the English in 1497 who technically first "discovered" the mainland United States. A man named John Cabot aboard a ship called the *Mathew* was the first to see land in what is now the United States of America. He sailed along the Eastern Seaboard of the United States, first spotting land at Cape Hatteras. Cabot was sponsored by Henry VIII, but the second Cornish uprising put a halt to any attempt to settle the continent at the time of Cabot's discovery.

In November 1577, Queen Elizabeth was presented with a document titled "A Discourse How Her Majesty May Annoy the King of Spaine by Fitting Out Shippes of War under Pretence of Letters Patent, to Discover and Inhabit Strange Places." This document in essence laid out a plan to loot Spanish ships under the guise of exploration, and if caught, the queen could deny any responsibility. She could support the "science" mission openly, and if those on her ships were caught stealing from the Spanish, she could pretend they acted on their own.

In 1578, Queen Elizabeth granted a patent to Sir Humphrey Gilbert, who made two voyages to the New World, neither of which was successful at establishing a colony. Gilbert was more concerned with finding a northwest passage to China than placing an English colony in America. He did make landfall in Newfoundland, Canada, and participated in quite a bit of pirating but never found a northwest passage nor successfully planted a colony. Gilbert's patent for exploration granted by Queen Elizabeth in 1578 was only for a six-year term. Thus, in 1583, his time was running out. This is when Gilbert set sail for the New World again with a fleet of five ships, one of which was under the command of his half brother Sir Walter Raleigh.

Raleigh and his ship had to turn back due to a lack of victuals, and they are probably lucky they did. Gilbert and his ship the *Squirrel* went down in a storm off Newfoundland with all hands lost.

After the tragic demise of Humphrey Gilbert, Sir Walter Raleigh would become the man who would launch the famous attempts at a colony in the New World. Queen Elizabeth I granted Raleigh a charter in his own name on New Year's Day, March 25, 1584. (The English celebrated New Year's on March 25 until 1752, when it was switched to January 1.) Coincidentally, the queen would die almost exactly nineteen years later, on March 24, 1602.

Spain was under the rule of King Philip II, who had been married to Queen Elizabeth's half sister Mary, now remembered as Bloody Mary. King Philip was Catholic and took extreme issue with Elizabeth, who was Protestant. Before England and Spain went to war, they were involved in proxy wars against each other. Spain aided Irish rebellions against England with guns, horses and money. England aided rebellions against Spain in the Netherlands with gunpowder, horses and cannons. Spain and England also stole ships from each other on the high seas but had yet to declare war in 1584. The Anglo-Spanish War technically was not declared until 1585, but everyone knew it was inevitable.

The Elizabethan Model

The English hoped to usher in a new model for settlement that would be far more humane than the Spanish model. The lands of the Natives were ravaged at a phenomenal rate by the Spanish, with around 3.5 million Natives burned alive, hanged, fed to dogs, beheaded, shot or killed by diseases within the first fifty years of exploration. Unlike the French and Spanish during this period, the English had a much more humanitarian approach to colonization in the New World, at least during Queen Elizabeth's rule. Their approach is known as the "Elizabethan model for Colonization." Elizabethans such as Richard Hakluyt, Thomas Harriot, John White and Sir Walter Raleigh believed Native Americans had been mistreated by the Spanish and pointed out how the Spanish abuse of Natives had led to Spain's downfall in its attempts to colonize the New World. The Elizabethans had a vision of colonizing the New World not by conquest but by trade and friendship.

RICHARD HAKLUYT WAS AN English geographer, author, clergyman and historian for all English voyages to the New World in the sixteenth century. After spending time in France learning all he could about the New World, Hakluyt published *Discourse Concerning Western Planting* in 1584, which pushed for a colony in the New World that would win American Indians over slowly by being kind and trading with them, as well as learning their languages and, above all, not treating them cruelly, as the Spanish unapologetically had done.

> *The Spaniards have exercised most outrageous and more than Turkish cruelties in all the West Indies, whereby they are everywhere there become most odious unto them who would join with us or any other most willingly to shake off their most intolerable yoke.*
>
> [The English should] *first learn the language of the people near adjoining (the gift of tongues being now taken away) and by little and little acquaint themselves with their manner and so with discretion and mildness distill into their purged minds the sweet and lively lines of the gospel.*

The Spanish had in fact fed babies to hunting dogs and hanged people thirteen at a time in a misguided effort to honor the apostles and Jesus. They also burned Natives alive and shoved stakes down their throats, cut open pregnant women with swords and drowned children. Christopher Columbus himself even wrote a letter to King Ferdinand of Spain describing how he purchased Native girls to use as sex slaves and how girls as young as nine and ten were in high demand. There is a reason American Indian groups across the United States protest Columbus Day every year and why many states have changed the day to Indigenous People's Day or Native American Day.

Richard Hakluyt was influenced by Bartholomew de las Cosas, a Spanish monk in the New World who had witnessed these atrocities and who vigorously spoke out against them. Spain eventually removed Columbus from power and put him in jail. The English Elizabethans, like Hakluyt and Harriot, were also appalled at these Spanish cruelties. They wanted to approach the New World and its peoples with a different way of thinking, a more humanitarian approach.

Along with the hope for an Elizabethan type of colony in the New World, England was also looking to find a way to raid Spanish shipping, and Hakluyt believed the New World was the weak spot of the Spanish empire: "If you touch him [King Philip II of Spain] in the [West] Indies, you touch the apple of his eye; for take away his treasure…[and] his old bands of soldiers will soon be dissolved, his purpose defeated, his power and strength diminished, his pride abated, and his tyranny utterly suppressed."

Hakluyt's lobbying for an English colony in the New World did not fall on deaf ears. In 1584, Queen Elizabeth issued the patent to settle the New World to Sir Walter Raleigh if for no other reason than to compete with England's mortal enemy, Spain, for wealth and resources. Sir Walter Raleigh (a famous English writer, poet, courtier and explorer) was given the task of finding a good settlement site in the New World to use as a base against Spanish shipping and to gain profit from trade and natural resources, just as Hakluyt had suggested in his *Discourse Concerning Western Planting*. Raleigh organized a recon mission to seek out just such a place. Hakluyt himself was planning to accompany the 1584 voyage, but for reasons that are unclear, he did not make the trip. Two ships captained by Philip Amadas and Arthur Barlowe embarked in April 1584, kicking off the first of the five Elizabethan voyages to the United States.

THE PRIMARY SOURCES

In addition to lobbying for an English colony in the New World, Hakluyt published *The Principal Navigations Voyages Traffiques & Discoveries of the English Nation*, which was a massive collection of handwritten accounts from the English explorers who came to the New World during the five sixteenth-century English voyages between 1584 and 1590. Almost everything we know about these voyages comes from Hakluyt's collection of these primary written accounts.

In addition to Hakluyt, Thomas Harriot was another important Elizabethan from whom we learn of the English voyages. Harriot was an amazing mathematician, astronomer and scientist; some call him the "Galileo of England." In 1585, Harriot accompanied the second Elizabethan voyage to the New World and lived there for a year before hitching a ride home with Francis Drake in 1586. During his year in the New World, Harriot kept journals about his experiences and observations of the Native people and their way of life. Upon returning to England, Harriot compiled his journals and wrote a beautiful ethnography of the Natives encountered by the English titled *A Brief and True Report of the New Found Land of Virginia*. Although the English were in North Carolina, all the land north of Florida was called Virginia by the English in the sixteenth century. Harriot's report is accompanied by the exquisitely detailed engravings of Theodor de Bry. De Bry based the engravings on the infamous watercolor paintings done by artist John White, who also accompanied the voyage in 1585 and returned to the New World again in 1587 and 1590. The written accounts collected by Hakluyt and Harriot together with the John White paintings are considered the ultimate primary sources for early Native life in the New World. These primary sources also provide an exquisitely detailed look at the voyages themselves and of the initial European-Native contact period. In order to understand the fate of the Lost Colony, it is important to know what happened in each voyage in order, starting with the first in 1584.

Chapter 2

THE FIRST VOYAGE

1584

In 1584, the English were at war with Spain. Spain was a military superpower, especially by sea, and with the profits from the New World, it had begun to raise a force to conquer the whole of England. Spain had colonies all over the Caribbean and had made a fortune in gold, sugar and other resources. It was theorized by the English military that raids could be made into the Caribbean to steal Spanish ships and deal a mighty blow in the war. A very successful raid had already been carried out in the Caribbean by English captain John Hawkins, resulting in the capture of a ship full of slaves. Sugar was worth as much as gold at the time, and the Caribbean had quickly been converted into a series of giant plantations of sugar by the Spanish.

Thus in 1584, Sir Walter Raleigh, under the patent from Queen Elizabeth, launched the first of the sixteenth-century English voyages to what is now the United States. This was a reconnaissance mission sent to find a naval base in the New World for privateers to launch raids against the Spanish. Queen Elizabeth I was to get 10 percent of all Spanish prizes, and only the Spanish were to be attacked. This was an opportunity for Englishmen to become extremely rich in very little time, and it helped the English overall in the war against Spain. The recon mission was also to note profitable natural resources and begin trade with whomever they met, but these goals were secondary to looting the Spanish.

In the sixteenth century, the square-rigged ships were dependent on major ocean currents to cross the Atlantic. Ships from Europe would follow the

Northern Equatorial Current down to the Caribbean and then would hook up with the Gulf Stream to go north to Croatoan, which would later take them all the way back northeast to Europe. It was better to capture Spanish ships on their way back to Europe rather than on their way to the Caribbean because the cargoes would be full of gold, silver and/or sugar.

The southern half of the Outer Banks was just what the English wanted in terms of looting the Spanish merchant ships. The Spanish colonies in Florida and the Caribbean followed the Gulf Stream current northeast to get back to Spain, and at no point is the land closer to this massive ocean current than at Croatoan. The islands of Hatteras and Ocracoke were used by pirates and privateers for centuries to come for this same reason. In order to rob a ship, one must be able to spot the ship. Croatoan and Wokokon (now Hatteras and Ocracoke) are the only places this can be accomplished because as soon as the Gulf Stream reaches the north end of Croatoan, it crashes headlong into the cold-water Labrador Current and turns violently to the east away from land.

The telescope and looking glass had not yet been invented, so people were limited to looking with the naked eye from an elevated position. There is a hill on Croatoan/Hatteras today that is sixty-six feet high, and one can see for a distance of thirty miles or more. The Gulf Stream is about half that distance.

In addition to this privateer base, any profitable resources were to be noted, as well as profitable trade with the Native population. Captains Philip Amadas and Arthur Barlowe set out in two ships, the *Admiral* and the *Roebuck*, to accomplish these objectives. They left England on April 27, 1584, and arrived at Croatoan on July 4, 1584. This recon mission of 1584 was made up of all men, and they stayed in the New World for only six weeks.

Barlowe's account of the voyage of 1584 is the first written record describing what is now known as the Outer Banks of North Carolina. Barlowe's account is included in Hakluyt's *Principal Navigations*.

ON JULY 4, 1584, Amadas and Barlowe crossed an inlet into the Pamlico Sound. Most likely, they crossed over an inlet named Chancandepeco, which no longer exists. The inlet Chancandepeco was located just north of the modern-day village of Buxton. The Algonquian word *Chancandepeco* means "that which is deep and becomes shallow." The inlets of the Outer Banks of

North Carolina are constantly shifting and changing, but they all lead from the deep ocean to the shallow sound.

When they entered this inlet, they stated it was a difficult entry, and they took a left and anchored in the sound off the shore a distance of three harquebus shots from the inlet. Many scholars enjoy debating where exactly Barlowe landed in 1584. The primary sources lend some fogginess to this debate because, unfortunately, Barlowe mistakenly wrote down the wrong name for where he first landed. He mistakenly called the place "Winganacoa," which actually means "you wear gay/happy clothes." The word, or rather the phrase, *winganacoa* was never misused again after 1584 because the English realized their mistake prior to the next voyage.

The English probably learned of the mistake from one of the two Natives they took home with them that year. Luckily, Barlowe was very descriptive about where he landed, and the geography of the Outer Banks is unique enough that it takes very little deduction to know he landed at Croatoan. However, one could reasonably make a case for Barlowe landing at Wokokon, modern-day Ocracoke.

Barlowe said they entered an inlet, took a left and landed on an island that was twenty miles long running from east to west and no more than six miles wide. He also stated that they could not see any land from this island.

The following is an excerpt from Barlowe: "We walked away from the shore toward the nearby hilltops; from this spot we could view the sea on both sides, to the north and to the south, as far as the eye could reach. The land stretched itself to the west, and we found later that it was an island only twenty miles long and not more than six miles wide."

Both Ocracoke and the lower half of Hatteras (which was its own island called Croatoan in the sixteenth century) are about twenty miles long from east to west. Both islands have a sea to the north and south from which you cannot see land. However, Ocracoke today is only one mile wide at the widest point and Hatteras is four miles wide at the town of Buxton. Both islands have experienced terrible erosion over the years, but four miles is much closer to the six miles Barlowe indicated, which supports the theory of landing at Croatoan.

Supporters of the Ocracoke-landing theory quote how Barlowe indicated that Wokokon was uninhabited, whereas Croatoan was not, and how Barlowe goes on to say that for the first two days they did not see anyone until Natives started to come over by canoe. This bit of evidence leans toward the first English landing in North America being at Wokokon because it would explain why they did not see anyone for two days. However, the Natives were likely cautious of these oddly dressed, strange people using guns, and it makes sense that the Natives would have waited a few days to approach them even if they were on their island home. In Barlowe's notes, he indicates that they did not go exploring very far in those first two days either, so it makes sense that they did not encounter the Native people. They did, however, see footprints—many of them—in those first few days.

One more piece of evidence for the Ocracoke-landing theorists is this: Richard Hakluyt wrote in the margin of Barlowe's account "Isle of Wokokon" next to Winganacoa to indicate that they first landed at Ocracoke. So it is possible that the first English voyage in 1584 with Amadas and Barlowe actually landed at Ocracoke, and after two days the Croatoan people canoed over from their adjoining island, Croatoan, and then they began their trade and friendship on the island of Wokokon (Ocracoke). Either way, the first encounter between English and Natives was with the Croatoan people of Hatteras Island.

It is important to clarify here that some scholars attempt to argue that Amadas and Barlowe first landed at Roanoke Island, which is impossible. One cannot land on Roanoke Island, spend a few weeks there and then next travel north to the island of Roanoke. Barlowe clearly states that after staying a few weeks on this island that he mistakenly called Winganacoa, he and seven other men headed north in the Pamlico Sound and then came to an island called Roanoke, where they spent one night and were treated kindly by the Natives there.

Here is an excerpt of Barlowe's exact words: "Myself, with 7 more went twenty miles into the river, that runneth toward the city of Skicoake (a town to the north near Chesapeake Bay, Virginia), which river they call Occam: and the following evening we came to an island called Roanoke, distance from the harbor by which we entered seven leagues."

So Barlowe clearly states that he left the island mistakenly labeled Winganacoa and went north to the island of Roanoke. Barlowe states they went a distance of seven leagues from the harbor in which they entered. In Old English, a nautical league was anywhere from 3.5 to 9.0 miles, so the distance is anywhere from 24.5 miles to 63.0 miles. The reason for this range is because a league was measured by how far they could see from their point of reference. If the observer was in a ship's nest, a league could have been as far as 9.0 miles. Some scholars get confused about this reference to leagues because they are measuring in terms of what a league means in today's language. In today's world, a nautical league is set at 3.5 miles. Scholars who are stuck on using modern-day measurements of a league argue that this indicates Barlowe originally entered at what is now referred to as Port Fernando and landed on modern-day Bodie Island, which was called Hatorask in 1584. However, Barlowe states very clearly that it took him two days to get to the isle of Roanoke from that harbor in which they entered, and it would only have taken an hour to get from Bodie Island to Roanoke, a distance of approximately 1.5 miles. Plus, Roanoke Island would have been easily visible from Hatorask/Bodie Island.

Barlowe stated that he could not see land from where he landed. Bodie Island also does not run east to west; it is in a north–south alignment. Bodie Island does not contain any high ground either, and Barlowe speaks of climbing a hill and firing a gun that caused an army of geese to fly up from the valley below. In other words, Bodie Island does not fit any of the criteria given in the primary sources, whereas Croatoan fits all of them and Wokokon fits most of them.

Hence, despite some "scholarly" arguments otherwise, the most logical conclusion is that Barlowe entered the inlet of Chancandepeco, turned left and landed on the island of Croatoan, which at the time was approximately twenty miles east to west, was approximately six miles wide and was/is a distance of approximately fifty miles from Roanoke Island (with a straight shot from Buxton to Wanchese). Landing at Croatoan also explains how the English met Manteo, a Croatoan man who returned to England with Barlowe. The main point of the mission was to find a good place to raid Spanish ships, and Croatoan was the only place close enough to spot Spanish ships in the Gulf Stream, which the Spanish used to sail home.

THE FIRST EVER MEETING between the English and Native Americans involved three curious Native men who took canoes to a point of land opposite where the English were anchored in the sound. One of the Natives came alongside the English ships by canoe, and the English invited this Native onto their ships, fed him and gave him gifts. They gave him wine, meat and some clothes. Immediately upon returning to the shore, this man fished for the English and left them two piles of fish, one for each ship.

Here it is described in Barlowe's exact words:

And after he had spoken of many things not understood by us, we brought him with his owne good liking, aboard the ships, and gave him a shirt, a hat & some other things, and made him taste of our wine, and our meat, which he liked very wel: and after having viewed both barks, he departed, and went to his owne boat againe, which hee had left in a little cove or creeke adjoining: as hee was two bow shots into the water, he fell to fishing and in less then halfe an houre, he had laden his boate as deepe, as it could swim, with which hee came againe to the point of lande, and there he divided his fish into two parts, pointing one part to the ship, and the other to the pinnesse.

In 1584, Barlowe made contact with at least two tribes, the Croatoan and the Secotan. The Secotan lived on the North Carolina mainland in a series of very small villages between the Pamlico River and the Roanoke River, as well as in a small village on Roanoke Island. The English got along with both tribes on this voyage and were showered with food and gifts everywhere they went. The English had some foreknowledge about what items they should bring to trade because of information Hakluyt had obtained from the French and Spanish. The Natives greatly desired English iron tools but also glass beads, copper and swords. The English were most impressed with the pearls, tobacco and leather of the Natives. Those on the 1584 recon mission were able to trade simple wares to get these goods.

Barlowe never met the Secotan chief Wingina nor the Croatoan chief Menatonan. He did, however, encounter Granganimeo, the brother of Wingina.

When we shewed him [Granganimeo] *all our packet of merchandize, of all things that he sawe, a bright tinne dish most pleased him, which hee presently tooke up and clapt it before his breast, and after made a hole in the brimme thereof and hung it about his necke, making signes that it would defende him against his enemies arrows.*

We exchanged our tinne dish for twentie skinnes.... They offered us good exchange for our hatchets and axes, and for our knives....He [Granganimeo] *himselfe had upon his head a broad plate of golde, or copper for being unpolished we knew not what metal it should be.*

Copper ornaments were worn by the political leaders and people of high status in Native societies all over the tidewater region of North Carolina and Virginia. They traded with other tribes farther inland to get the copper, and it was valued much the way gold was by Europeans. One copper pot was traded for fifty deerskins. A mere ten deerskins were worth a year's salary for an English sailor. Barlowe had not found gold or silver, but he had found very profitable trade and, more importantly, a good place to loot Spanish ships.

Barlowe, as instructed, also noted the bountiful resources of the Natives:

> He [Granganimeo] *sent us every day a brace or two of fat bucks, conies, hares, fish, the best of the world. He sent us divers kinds of fruits, melons, walnuts, cucumbers, gourds, peas, and divers roots and fruits very excellent good, and of their country corn, which is very white, fair, and well tasted, and groweth three times in five months....Only they cast the corn into the ground, breaking a little of the soft turf with a wooden mattock or pickaxe. Ourselves proved the soil and put some of our peas into the ground, and in ten days they were of fourteen inches high. They have also beans very fair, of divers colours and wonderful plenty, some growing naturally, and some in their gardens, and so have they both wheat and oats.*

Barlowe was told by two Natives named Manteo and Wanchese about a shipwreck that, according to the Natives, occurred twenty years earlier and was described by Barlowe as a ship from some other "Christian nation." The iron spikes had been taken out of the wreck and used as tools by the tribe for all that time. Barlowe tells of this story here when the two Natives were describing how they made their canoes:

> *Their boats are made of one tree, either pine or of pitch trees: a wood not commonly knowne to our people, nor found growing in England. They have no edged tools to make them withal: if they have any they are very fewe, and those it seems they had twentie years since, which as those two* [to] *me* [Manteo and Wanchese] *declared, was out of a wracke which happened upon their coast of some Christian shippe, being beaten that way by some storme, and outrageous weather, whereof none of the people were saved but only the shippe or some part of her, being cast upon the sand, out of whose sides they drewe the nails and spikes and with those made their best instruments.*

The shipwreck was probably Spanish or French in origin, but we will never know for sure. Iron axes, saws and tools were heavily valued by all the tribes Barlowe met. The iron tools greatly eased tilling the land and the building of houses and canoes for the Natives. Prior to iron tools, the Natives had to burn trees to the ground rather than cut them and then burn and scrape the charred trees with shell tools to build a canoe. This process for canoe building was very labor intensive and no doubt time consuming. It is possible that this wreck is the same one that Barlowe heard about later from the Indians on Roanoke, although they said it was twenty-six years prior instead of twenty and they said there were two survivors rather than none.

Barlowe's written account of this shipwreck as told to him by the Natives in Roanoke is as follows:

> *Towards the sunset four days' journey is situate a town called Sequotan, which is the westernmost town of Wingandacoa, near unto which, six-and-twenty years past, there was a ship cast away, whereof some of the people were saved, and those were white people whom the country people preserved. And after ten days, remaining in an out-island uninhabited called Wococon, they, with the help of some of the dwellers of Sequotan, fastened two boats of the country together and made masts unto them and sails of their shirts, and, having taken into them such victuals as the country yielded, they departed after they had remained in this out-island three weeks. But shortly after, it seemed, they were cast away, for the boats were found upon the coast, cast aland in another island adjoining. Other than these, there was never any people apparelled or white of colour either seen or heard of amongst these people.*

If these castaways attempted to make another ship out of what they had at hand and the remains of this makeshift ship washed up on an island that was next to Wokokon (Croatoan), then it would make sense that Manteo, who was Croatoan, reported no survivors and that only the wreck was found, from which they took the metal spikes. This also supports the theory of Barlowe landing at Croatoan, as Manteo was discussing the shipwreck on his island while Barlowe was on the island he had mistakenly called "Winganacoa."

Barlowe and his crew spent six weeks in the New World and established good trade relations with the Natives and found a perfect place to spot Spanish ships. When Barlowe returned to England, he presented the fine deerskins, pearls, tobacco and other items acquired through trade. He also brought back the Natives Manteo and Wanchese, who were described as "lusty fellows." These men were basically used as male models, living props paraded around and even taken to the queen's court to entice investors for a return voyage. They must have made the deerskin clothes look great because a majority of the investors for the second voyage were leather merchants.

THERE ARE NO DETAILED primary records of the journey back to England in 1584. Barlowe is the only surviving source we have for the 1584 voyage, and his report ends before the journey home. The next voyage to the Outer Banks from England departed in the spring of 1585 and lasted a year. The two main primary sources for the 1585 voyage come from Sir Richard Grenville and Ralph Lane. Grenville was the admiral in charge of a fleet of seven ships, and Lane was a military captain who would end up being in charge of 105 men who stayed in the New World a little over a year. The next primary source available after Barlowe is the ship log of the *Tiger*, one of seven ships to return to the New World in the spring of 1585.

We have no detailed primary source or written record of the Native men's time in England, but we do know that they were presented at Queen Elizabeth's court and given gifts. We also know that they stayed with Thomas Harriot.

Chapter 3

THE SECOND VOYAGE

1585–1586

The details of the 1585 voyage to America are found in accounts written by Captain Grenville himself and Ralph Lane's written account. In addition, an unknown passenger of the *Tiger* kept a journal of the 1585 trip, which Hakluyt also later added to his collection in *Principal Navigations*.

❦

SEVEN SHIPS MADE UP the second English voyage to the New World, all owned by private investors except one. The queen was willing to part with one ship and required a percentage of any profits made from plundering the Spanish. This ship was the largest ship of the seven and was called the *Tiger*. It was built by Queen Elizabeth's father, Henry VIII, and carried nearly half of the six hundred total men to make the journey. Queen Elizabeth also authorized the use of four hundred pounds of gunpowder from the Tower of London for the journey. This powder was not meant for killing Indians but rather Spaniards. The English were making a serious and bold attempt to strike the Spanish in the soft underbelly of its colonies, just as advocated by Richard Hakluyt.

So it was on April 9, 1585, that the second English voyage to the New World set sail. This English fleet making its way to the New World was headed by Sir Richard Grenville, a cousin of Sir Walter Raleigh. Both Manteo and Wanchese were onboard the *Tiger*, heading home to Croatoan.

In addition to the *Tiger*, there was the *Roebuck*, the *Red Lyon*, the *Elizabeth*, the *Dorothy* and two small pinnaces.

The route to the New World from England followed the natural ocean currents, primarily the Northern Equatorial Current and the Gulf Stream. If the wind slacked off, the ships could at least drift in the right direction with the current. Fish also follow these currents, which made them good places to catch fish and turtles. The fish were a welcome supplement to the salted pork and sea biscuits the English had to suck down for months at a time. It was very difficult to keep most foods from spoiling, and therefore, things like fruit and vegetables had to be eaten immediately and resupplied along the way from various islands. Even water would spoil on the hot ships, and thus the poor sailors were forced to drink beer on a daily basis.

About a week into the voyage, off the coast of Portugal, a bad storm blew in and the ships were all scattered. The next morning, the *Tiger* found itself all alone. In those days, there was no way to contact a ship that was out of sight other than fire a cannon and hope the other ship heard it. Therefore, when a fleet was scattered, the ships would rendezvous at the final destination. During the storm, unbeknownst to Grenville, one of the smaller ships landed at Portugal and discontinued the journey. The *Tiger* also lost a small ship it had in tow during the storm.

The *Tiger* and crew continued on and next stopped at Tallaboa Bay, Puerto Rico, which was held by the Spanish at the time. While in Puerto Rico, the English from the *Tiger* built another small ship from timber found on the island to replace the one lost. They also built a fort, which the Spanish burned after Grenville departed. It was at Puerto Rico that the men from the *Tiger* reconnected with one of the other ships from the fleet, the *Elizabeth*. Together, the *Elizabeth*, the *Tiger* and the newly built, unnamed ship sailed, stopping to raid a Spanish saltworks en route to the Outer Banks. The *Tiger* also sacked two Spanish ships on the way and put prize crews on them to sail back to England. They ransomed the Spanish officers for pigs and "goodly" sums of money. Due to the extra time spent looting the Spanish, the *Tiger* was actually the last ship of the original seven to arrive at the Outer Banks.

Captain Raymond, who was in charge of the English fleet's second-largest ship, called the *Red Lyon*, was the first to arrive at the Outer Banks, a full three weeks ahead of Grenville and the *Tiger*. Captain Raymond was eager to drop off his share of the men for the military outpost and continue north to loot ships. He left his soldiers with the Croatoan, which is very telling, for it clearly demonstrates that Croatoan was the fleet's final destination and rendezvous point. Raymond left his men on Croatoan, where the base camp of the previous voyage made by Barlowe a year earlier had been located. He knew this was the place the rest of the fleet was headed and thus the men he left would reconnect with Grenville and the others. These thirty-two men who had already gone ashore began construction of a series of forts along the beach guarding the inlets of the Outer Banks. They also spent their time at Croatoan trading goods, shooting birds and catching fish. The Croatoan shared their food and treated the English like brothers.

In June 1585, Grenville and the *Tiger* finally arrived. The English had made a great profit at the expense of the Spanish on the way over, but luck was about to run out. On June 29, 1585, the *Tiger* ran aground off Ocracoke/Wokokon, a fitting welcome to the Outer Banks (now known as the Graveyard of the Atlantic for thousands of shipwrecks that forever rest there). The *Tiger* had the lion's share of the English supplies, not to mention all the stolen goods from the Spanish. The wreck caused the loss of a lot of supplies and even caused the men on the *Tiger* to have to throw the horses overboard in order to lighten the load and try to get free of the bar. Some say this is how the wild horses ended up on Ocracoke—the few that made it to shore.

While stranded on the sandbar, Grenville decided to split up a few of his men from the *Tiger*, sending one group up to Croatoan and another group to the mainland. Grenville stayed with the *Tiger* until it was lightened enough to be free of the sandbar. This was what was reported back to him and written in Grenville's diary: "The 6th [July] M. John Arundel was sent to the main, and Manteo with him: and Captain Aubry and Captain Boniten the same day were sent to Croatoan, where they found two of our men left there with 30 others by Captain Reymond, some 20 days before."

The shipwreck of the *Tiger* greatly altered the English plans and quite possibly changed the course of history altogether. The *Tiger* was freed from the bar, but with a great loss of cargo. As a direct result of this, Grenville determined he must make up for all the losses, and he left the Outer Banks with 495 of the 600 men and all the large ships to raid the Spanish Azores. He left behind 105 soldiers under the direction of Ralph Lane, a ruthless, harsh commander who should never have been in charge if Hakluyt's vision of mutually benefiting societies was to be reached. Lane and Grenville were also bitter rivals, and had this shipwreck never occurred and Grenville had been able to stay, the course of history most certainly would have been different.

The 1585 voyage was not an attempt at putting a permanent English settlement in the New World. The group did not include any women. Their mission was to loot and harm the Spanish in any way possible. Croatoan is the only place high enough and close enough to the Gulf Stream to see the Spanish ships coming from Florida and the Caribbean en route to Spain, laden with treasures from the New World. Croatoan was used by pirates and later lifesaving stations to spot ships for centuries. Secondary to setting up a base to loot the Spanish was making a profit through trade with the Native populations and taking advantage of any and all natural resources they could find. These were the goals in 1585—not a settlement or colony.

Grenville would capture a Spanish ship full of silver off Bermuda during his return trip for a great profit. He was in the New World for less than two months. The *Tiger* ran aground on June 29 and departed on August 25. There was no mention of Roanoke Island until August 24, so Grenville never even went there.

With Grenville gone and Ralph Lane now in charge, the honeymoon period between the Natives and the English that had started in 1584 was about to change. The trouble began at a Secotan village called Aguscogoc, located near modern-day Scranton, North Carolina. The English noticed a silver cup had been stolen after visiting this town, and as punishment, Philip Amadas and sixteen others were sent to burn the village and the adjoining grain fields to the ground, which they did. The English were now involved in a conflict with the Secotan, who were also the traditional rival of the Croatoan. In 1585, Croatoan chief Menatonan was still recovering from wounds he got from fighting with the Secotan. According to Barlowe:

> *The King himself in person was at our being there, sore wounded in a fight which he had with the King of the next country, called Wingina, and was shot in two places through the body, and once clean through the thigh, but yet he recovered: by reason whereof and for that he lay at the chief town of the country, being six days journey off, we saw him not at all.*

Barlowe was mistaken in calling the next country or neighboring country Wingina, but he was not too far off, for Wingina was the name of the chief of that country. We also learn from primary accounts that came after Barlowe that the name of the chief who was wounded fighting against the land of Wingina was Menatonan. Menatonan was met on the second English voyage to the New World (1585) a great distance from Croatoan, perhaps six days away by the method used by the Natives, which would have been by canoe. He was wounded and unable to walk and was in the largest town the English visited (chief town of the country). An undisputed expert on the

Elizabethan voyages, David Beers Quinn recognized that Menatonan was "apart from Manteo, the only member of the Croatoan tribe to be named. He was evidently a prominent person in the tribe."

I would go one further than Quinn and suggest Menatonan was in fact the Croatoan chief. Menatonan was betrayed by Wingina, who tried to instigate a fight between him and the English. Wingina sent the English to Chowan, promising great trade in pearls, and then sent word ahead of the English to tell Menatonan the English were coming to destroy him and that he should raise an army to destroy the English first. The trick worked. Menatonan had men ready to attack the English, who, upon seeing this, fired scattershot at them from small cannons. The English did not discover Wingina's treachery until they had already attacked and captured Menatonan. Lane spent two days talking with Menatonan and said he was very wise. The name Menatonan means "he who listens well." Menatonan told Lane that Wingina had sent him word that a greater enemy faced them both and that he should destroy them. Lane said he had only come to trade. Lane did not know if Menatonan was telling the truth, so he took Menatonan's son Skico as a prisoner and demanded tribute be paid to him in grain. Menatonan regularly delivered food to Lane at Roanoke Island after this and insisted it was all Wingina's fault they had fought.

While Lane, Manteo and about forty soldiers were on their trip to Chowan and away from Secotan lands, Wingina tore up fishing weirs they had previously built for the English on Roanoke Island. Wingina also had his allies the Mandoag ambush the English on the Chowan River during the English return voyage from Chowan near modern-day Colerain, North Carolina. The Mandoag showered the English ship with arrows from both sides of the river and then ran off. The Mandoag reported falsely that they had killed the English, so when Lane and his men returned unharmed, some in Wingina's council thought they had risen from the dead. They believed that once killed, the English slowly drained the life out of healthy Natives until they died, and then the English took that life force and rose from the dead. Part of this belief came from the fact that so many Natives had died from English diseases, including Wingina's brother Granganimeo and his father, Ensanore. They had never known disease and could not explain why so many fell weak and died. It was Ensanore who had argued not to antagonize the English, while Wingina had argued to attack and kill all the English. Wanchese, who also hated the English, was living in Dasamonquepue with Wingina. Once Ensanore died, there was no one left in the council to argue not to kill the English.

It was later revealed to Lane by none other than Skico (whom Lane had released) that Wingina had a plan to starve the English until they spread out and then attack them one group at a time by burning their houses and then ambushing the men as they ran out of them. Lane commented:

> *In the dead time of the night they* [Secotan] *would have beset my house, and put fire in the reeds that the same was covered with: meaning (as it was likely) that myself would have come running out of a sudden amazed in my shirt without arms, upon the instant whereof they would have knocked out my brains. The same order was given to certain of his fellows, for M. Heriots: so for all the rest of our better sort, all our houses at one instant being set on fire as afore is said, and that as well for them of the fort, as for us at the town.*

It is a common misconception that the fort and settlement sites on Roanoke Island were one and the same. Ralph Lane makes it clear that the fort and settlement were not in the same location. John White also indicates the fort was some distance from the town.

The first phase of Wingina's plan to refuse to feed the English and starve them until they spread out worked; Lane and his men were reduced to eating their own hunting dogs at one point. They also had indeed spread out, with ten men sent to Hatorask (Bodie Island), fifteen sent to the mainland and twenty sent to Croatoan to feed themselves and spot ships so that they might be resupplied. Lane continued:

> *For the famine grew so extreme among us, our weirs failing us of fish, that I was enforced to send Captain Stafford with 20 with him to Croatoan my Lord Admirals Island to serve two turns in one, that is to say, to feed himself and his company, and also to keep watch if any shipping came upon the coast to warn us of the same.*

The Englishmen living at Croatoan did spot a fleet of ships that turned out to be that of Sir Francis Drake, who would rescue the English and take them back to England. Unfortunately, this was not accomplished before Ralph Lane, a group of English soldiers and Manteo with his friends ambushed and killed the Secotan chief, Wingina, and members of his council. Wingina was shot twice and recovered both times to get up and flee. In the end, an Irishman cut off his head.

Lane explained:

> *I went to Dasamonquepeio: I gave the watch-word agreed upon, (which was, Christ our victory) and immediately those his chief men and himself had by the mercy of God for our deliverance, that which they had purposed for us. The king himself being shot throw by the Colonel with a pistol, lying on the ground for dead, & I looking as watchfully for the saving of Manteo's friends, as others were busy that none of the rest should escape, suddenly he started up, and ran away as though he had not been touched, insomuch as he overran all the company, being by the way shot thwart the buttocks by mine Irish boy with my petronell. In the end an Irish man serving me, one Nugent, and the deputy provost, undertook him; and following him in the woods, overtook him: and I in some doubt least we had lost both the king & my man by our own negligence to have been intercepted by the savages, we met him returning out of the woods with Pemisapan's head in his hand.*

Wingina had changed his name to Pemisapan after the deaths of his brother Granganimeo and father, Ensanore. *Dasamonquepeu* is a Carolina Algonquian word that means "peninsula" and was spelled differently each time the English wrote it down. It was also the name of a mainland town where Mann's Harbor, North Carolina, is today.

It was not long after the English ambushed and killed Wingina/Pemisapan at Dasamonquepeu that the English who had been sent to live at Croatoan with Captain Stafford spotted an English fleet. Edward Stafford reported to Ralph Lane that Sir Francis Drake had arrived at Croatoan and was willing to resupply Lane and his 105 weary soldiers. At first, Lane wanted to remain in the New World and asked only for supplies. Drake packed everything Lane asked for, including more men, onto a ship called the *Francis*. A storm hit and drove the *Francis* far out to sea, forcing Lane to relinquish his desire to stay and instead return to England with Drake. Lane also had a chest of pearls fall overboard.

The burning down of the village Aguscogoc was the beginning of a downward spiral for English-Secotan relations. The Croatoan, on the other hand, remained friendly to the English and would later capitalize on the weakened Secotan nation. Sometimes the Croatoan are mistaken as part of the Secotan tribe, which they clearly were not. This will be demonstrated best in chapter 5.

LANE AND HIS MEN spent almost a year in the New World. Lane blamed the lack of supplies and food for the failure of the mission. Many others, including Grenville, blamed Lane's cruelty to the Natives.

The queen supported Grenville because he had been very successful against the Spanish during and between his voyages. When he left the New World in 1585 on board the *Tiger*, he captured a Spanish galleon full of silver off the coast of Bermuda. This ship made Grenville enough money to pay off the entire cost of the 1585 voyage and then some.

Lane departed in shame with Drake. Little did he know that Grenville's resupply ships were almost there.

Chapter 4

THE RESUPPLY MISSION

1586

Ironically, a week after Lane and his men left the New World with Drake, a supply ship sent by Sir Walter Raleigh arrived. The resupply mission was late in arriving because it had been delayed by the very same storm that sank the *Francis* and swiped Lane's chests of pearls. When Raleigh's men arrived at Roanoke, they saw no one and headed back home to England.

Two weeks after Raleigh's supply ships left, Grenville returned to Roanoke with three ships laden with even more supplies. Grenville's men had no way of knowing the terrible situation they were walking into. Lane had left the Secotan with a murdered chief, a village and its fields burned to the ground and diseases that had killed the chief's father, Ensenore, and his brother Granganimeo, among many others.

When Grenville returned to the New World, he was dumbfounded. He landed at Hatorask and saw no signs of any men. He looked at Roanoke as well and found it abandoned. He did not want to lose the land they had held for such a long time, so he decided to leave fifteen men on Roanoke Island with enough supplies to last them for two years. They were to live in the houses left behind by the departed settlement and garrison the little fort there.

Grenville left and headed toward the Spanish-held Azores. As always, he was very successful in his raids of the Azores, capturing much bounty, which he knew would please Queen Elizabeth. They stole everything, even the door hinges.

Back in Roanoke, the fifteen men left behind were about to pay for the mistakes Lane and his soldiers had made. Word spread quickly among the Natives that more white men had returned. With Wingina, Ensenore and Granganimeo all dead, the Secotan Natives wanted revenge and needed a fierce leader to take it. Historians have speculated that Wanchese may have taken this role because he was part of Wingina/Pemesipan's council, but it could have been any of the surviving councilmen or someone from outside the council who took over after Wingina was killed.

The fifteen English soldiers left behind were attacked by Secotan warriors from Dasamonquepeu. At least two were killed, and the others fled east from Roanoke Island in a small boat, never to be seen or heard from again.

Chapter 5

THE "LOST" COLONY

1587

The fourth English voyage to the New World was the only one meant to last. Therefore, it was the first English voyage to bring women and children. The three previous voyages were military operations and established trade outposts. Even though the English military had found an excellent coastline for privateering the Spanish, the 1587 colony was not looking to loot ships. This group was looking for a deep harbor to set up a thriving port town. The transatlantic ships of the sixteenth century had deep drafts, and as such, they could not easily get in and out of the shallow sound around Roanoke Island. For this reason, the 1587 colony actually planned to settle farther north in the Chesapeake Bay area, which had a deeper harbor and reports of larger pearls. It was a perfect place to set up a port town. The colonists planned to briefly stop by Roanoke just long enough to pick up the fifteen men left there by Grenville the year before. Remember, they had no idea the fate that had befallen Grenville's fifteen soldiers. This was their plan, but almost nothing went right on this voyage from the beginning to the end. Simon Fernando, who was an excellent pilot but a former pirate, was selected to guide the colony to the New World; however, his actions ultimately proved that he was intent on sabotaging the success of the colony.

In the spring of 1587, at the start of the new year, the fourth English voyage to the New World embarked on its journey. It should be noted that New Year's prior to 1742 was celebrated on March 25, not January 1. For those unaware of this fact, the English dates can be confusing.

The voyage consisted of three ships: the *Lion*, which was piloted by Fernando; a flyboat commanded by Captain Spicer (a good friend of John White); and a pinnace commanded by Captain Stafford. Sir Walter Raleigh appointed John White as the governor of the colony and named the new land Virginia, after Queen Elizabeth, the virgin queen. John White also brought his pregnant daughter Eleanor Dare with him and her husband, Ananias Dare. Manteo was again with the voyage returning to the New World, and by this time, he had developed very good English and would serve well as an interpreter. He had also become friends with many of the English. In total, 117 men, women and children set out on this voyage to the New World to set up a new way of life and a port town for the English to use on their travels to and from the New World.

Before diving into the details of the voyage and the colony itself, it is important to understand the dynamics of the Native people whom the colonists were about to encounter. Too often, authors and historians from the twentieth century paint the Natives with too large a brush, lumping them all together into one massive tribe and making no distinction between them as separate nations. Instead, they are just referred to in one category as "Indians." These same authors and historians tend to ignore the impact that the Natives had on this time in history and focus solely on the English perspective. It is this kind of dismissive attitude toward the Native tribes and their influence that has made so many "scholars" blind to understanding the fate of the 1587 colony.

The Croatoan are often mistaken as part of the Secotan tribe and/or are mistaken as being friendly with the Secotan tribe. The primary sources make it very clear that this was not the case. To begin with, Manteo tells the members of the 1584 voyage about how a neighboring tribe killed many of his tribe in 1582 through trickery. It is also demonstrated plainly throughout the primary sources that the Croatoan were never with Wingina or the Secotan. In fact, there is a direct quote where the Croatoan tell John White in 1587 that they want to wear badges or tokens to show that they are not Secotan, not their enemy.

It also becomes clear from White's 1587 account that Menatonan was definitely the chief of the Croatoan. In 1584, Barlowe mentions that the chief of the Croatoan is in the largest town, which is six days' journey from Croatoan, and that he is there recovering from a wound he obtained while fighting against the neighboring tribe (Secotan) that has left him lame (unable to walk). In 1585, during Lane's journey up the river to Chowanoke, the largest town he encounters, he finds a wounded chief named Menatonan who is unable to walk.

Menatonan was clearly Wingina's enemy in 1585–86. Remember that Wingina tried to instigate a fight between the English and Menatonan by telling Ralph Lane that the Chowanoke wished to kill him and his men. Ultimately, Skico, who is Menatonan's son, told Lane of Wingina's plan to kill Lane and his men through starvation (even though Skico is Lane's prisoner). This clearly shows Skico and Menatonan's hatred of the Secotan and Wingina. In addition, in 1587, Menatonan's wife and baby were found with the Croatoan tribe raiding the fields of Wingina's old town Dasamonquepeu.

There are many quotes from the primary accounts that accentuate this point that the Secotan and the Croatoan were enemies and that the Croatoan were always friendly to the English. Understanding that the Croatoan and Secotan are two different tribes is critical to understanding the events that unfolded in 1587 and the ultimate fate of the colony.

A quote from John White in 1587 emphasizes this point. Here he is discussing the Croatoan tribe:

> *Our coming was only to renew the old love, that was between us and them at the first, and to live with them as brethren and friends: which answer seemed to please them well, wherefore they requested us to walk up to their town, who there feasted us after their manner, and desired us earnestly, that there might be some token or badge given them of us, whereby we might know them to be our friends, when we met them anywhere out of the town or island.*

In 1587, the Croatoan even complained to White that some of their men had been mistaken for Wingina's men and attacked by the Lane settlement. One Croatoan male was made lame from it.

This is another direct quote from White:

> *They* [Croatoan] *told us further that for want of some such badge, diverse of them were hurt the year before, being found out of the island by master Lane his company, whereof they showed us one which at the very instant lay lame and had lien of that hurt ever since: but they said they knew our men mistook them and hurt them instead of Wingina's men whereof they held us excused.*

What the English really wanted to know was what had happened to the fifteen men left on Roanoke in 1586. Here is the excerpt from White:

We understood by them of Croatoan, how that the 15 Englishmen left at Roanoak the year before, by Sir Richard Grenville, were suddenly set upon, by 30 of the men of Secota, Aquascogoc, and Dasamonguepek, in manner following. They conveyed themselves secretly behind the trees, near the houses where our men carelessly lived: and having perceived that of those fifteen they could see but eleven only, two of those Savages appeared to the 11 Englishmen, calling to them by friendly signs, that but two of their chiefest men should come unarmed to speak with those two savages, who seemed also to bee unarmed. Wherefore two of the chiefest of our Englishmen went gladly to them: but whilst one of those savages traitorously embraced one of our men, the other with his sword of wood, which he had secretly hidden under his mantel, struck him on the head and slew him, and presently the other eight and twenty savages showed themselves: the other Englishman perceiving this, fled to his company, whom the savages pursued with their bows, and arrows, so fast, that the Englishmen were forced to take the house, wherein all their victual, and weapons were: but the savages, forthwith set the same on fire: by means whereof our men were forced to take up such weapons as came first to hand, and without order to run forth among the savages, with whom they skirmished above an hour. In this skirmish another of our men was shot into the mouth with an arrow, where he died: and also one of the Savages was shot into the side by one of our men, with a wild fire arrow, whereof he died presently.

White goes on to report how nine Englishmen out of the eleven attacked fled and met up with the other four Englishmen who had been fishing in a small boat. Together, they all fled east in the boat and were never seen again. He also said the fort had been destroyed.

When we came thither, we found the fort razed down, but all the houses standing unhurt, saving that the nether rooms of them, and also of the fort, were overgrown with melons of diverse sorts, and deer within them, feeding on those melons: so we returned to our company, without hope of ever seeing any of the fifteen men living.

So what happened to these fifteen men? According to the Croatoan, two of them were killed by the Secotan. Did the others attempt to sail home and perish? Did they all eventually meet their demise the same way as the other two in their party? Did they starve? No one knows, as the Croatoan reported to White in 1587 that they did not know what happened to those thirteen men after they fled in a small boat.

There are some later reports from Jamestown that mention Powhatan's tribe killing some Englishmen and saving their helmets as proof. Could the men whom Powhatan killed have been the thirteen men left by Grenville, rather than men from the 1587 colony, since Powhatan did not mention any women or children? In addition, the helmets are more indicative of Grenville's men because helmets are something soldiers wear, not civilians, and the 1587 colony was made up of civilians. There is also serious doubt that the reported slaughter ever happened because the source comes from an overtly racist minister who wrote in an anti-Indian pamphlet that John Smith told him that Smith had been told by Indians of the slaughter of the colony. Smith never mentions anything about this in any of his books.

The Lost Colony arrived at Roanoke Island to pick up Grenville's fifteen men only to find an unburied, dried-up skeleton and a burned fort with reports of an attack by the Secotan that killed at least two of the fifteen men. Then it got even worse for the English. A colonist by the name of George Howe was alone crabbing in the sound and was shot sixteen times with arrows and had his head smashed. John White reported:

> *The eight and twentieth, George Howe, one of our twelve assistants was slain by diverse savages, which were come over to Roanoke, either of purpose to spy our company, and what number we were, or else to hunt deer, whereof were many [deer] in the Island. These savages being secretly hidden among high reeds, where oftentimes they find the deer asleep, and so kill them, spied our man wading in the water alone, almost naked, without any weapon, save only a small forked stick, catching crabs therewithal, and also being strayed two miles from his company, and shot at him in the water, where they gave him sixteen wounds with their arrows: and after they had slain him with their wooden swords, they beat his head in pieces, and fled over the water to the main.*

After the murder of George Howe and the apparent demise of the fifteen soldiers left the year before, the English colony turned to Manteo and the Croatoan for help. Manteo, who had just returned to the New World, completing his second round trip across the Atlantic Ocean, was ready to see his home and family again. Governor White sent Edward Stafford and Manteo to Croatoan to ask about George Howe and the fifteen men from the year before. Stafford had lived on Croatoan for months under the Lane expedition and was well known to the Croatoan people as a friend. White continued:

> *On the thirtieth of July, Master Stafford and twenty of our men passed by water to the Island of Croatoan, with Manteo, who had his mother, and many of his kindred dwelling in that island, of whom we hoped to understand some news of our fifteen men, but especially to learn the disposition of the people of the country towards us, and to renew our old friendship with them.*

When they arrived at Croatoan, the Natives there hosted the English to a feast. They told the English it was the Secotan who had done the killings, which was a shock to no one. White explained, "We understood of the men of Croatoan, that our man Master Howe was slain by the remnant of Wingina's men dwelling then at Dasamonguepeu, with whom Wanchese kept company."

The English also asked the Croatoan to help them negotiate peace with the Secotan. The English asked the Croatoan to tell the Secotan they would forgive the killing of George Howe and the two men the year before if the Secotan were willing to forgive them for Lane's horrid behavior. They instructed the Croatoan to tell the Secotan leaders that they could send word back through the Croatoan or come to Roanoke themselves with their answer. The English gave a deadline of one week, after which time if no word was heard, they would assume the Secotan were still their enemies and would attack them. The Croatoan agreed to help the English.

After the one-week deadline had passed and the English had heard nothing from the Secotan (not by way of the Croatoan or directly), they did exactly what they promised and brought a force over to Dasamonquepeu in the dead of night to attack. What the English did not know was that the Secotan had already fled farther inland, and the Croatoan were in Dasamonquepeu stealing all of the crops that had been left behind by the Secotan. The English almost attacked the Croatoan, who avoided disaster because one of them knew Captain Stafford by name and called out to him. Manteo, being with the English during the raid, chastised his Native brothers and sisters for not sending some sort of word to them at Roanoke before the appointed date. Luckily, a huge disaster was avoided. Menatonan's wife and baby, who were there collecting crops with the other Natives, were given a ride on an English lightship to Roanoke, and the spoils of Dasamonquepeu were shared between the English and the Croatoan.

During John White's short stay at Roanoke before heading home to resupply, he experienced many happy moments as well. His granddaughter Virginia Dare was born with the infamous designation as the first English child born in the New World. Another English child only listed as Baby Harvie was also born during those few short weeks. Manteo was baptized as a Christian, the first Native American to be baptized by the English, and he was given the title Lord of Roanoke and Dasamonquepeu (even though he was a Croatoan). The title served to show that the Croatoan now owned and controlled these lands, Roanoke and Dasamonquepeu.

At this point, you may be asking yourself, why have the colonists not left yet for Chesapeake? Why are they still on Roanoke? They only went there to find the fifteen men from the year before and never planned to stay. Alas, the pirate Simon Fernando had his own mission. Fernando did many treacherous things attempting to make the colony fail. One of the biggest was when he refused to take the colony farther north to their intended destination of Chesapeake Bay. It was only after Governor White and the colonists had departed from the ships in small boats that Simon Fernando informed White he would not sail to the Chesapeake Bay because it was too late in the season. The English, as well as the French and Spanish, tried to avoid sailing in the Atlantic Ocean during late summer and early fall because that is hurricane season, which they called the tempest.

From White's account:

> But as soone as we were put with our pinnesse from the ship, Ferdinando [sic], who was appointed to returne for England called to the sailors in the pinnesse, charging them not to bring any of the planters backe againe, but to leave them in the Island of Roanoke, except the Governour, & two or three such as he approved, saying that the summer was farre spent, wherefore he would land all the planters in no other place.

Fernando had also secretly informed an Irishman by the name of Darby Glande of his plot to abandon the colony at Roanoke rather than take them to the Chesapeake as planned. (You have to remember Irishmen were generally slaves to the English in the sixteenth century, so there was no love lost between Darby Glande and the English.) When they stopped at Santa Cruz on the way to the New World, Darby and another Irishman disappeared from the ship and made their way to the nearest Spanish town. Darby informed the Spanish that the colonists were going to Roanoke. One can only deduce that Fernando must have instructed Darby to inform the Spanish, in hopes that they would attack England's precious colony. Sadly for Darby Glande, it is unknown what riches may have been promised to him by Fernando for this obedient act, but his fate actually made him a prisoner of the Spanish for the next seven years as an oarsman for a galley. Ouch.

So the colony was left at Roanoke, not Chesapeake, and landed in the midst of the angry Secotan tribe, and unbeknownst to them, the Spanish in the Caribbean had been informed of their whereabouts by the traitorous pirate Simon Fernando. A daytime soap opera could not come up with more drama!

With a heavy heart, John White was forced to return home with Simon Fernando. He promised to come back quickly with supplies. He informed his family and the planters to carve into a tree, palisade or other obvious location where they relocated to and to carve a cross under the name if they had to leave for reasons of danger. He also buried a chest of some of his personal items on Roanoke Island before he left.

As his daughter Eleanor, his son-in-law Ananias and his granddaughter Virginia, along with the other 1587 colonists, bid him goodbye with a wave and prayers for a safe journey, they were all ignorant of the fact that it would be three long years before Governor White would return to Roanoke. And it was lost on all of them that they were ultimately being abandoned forever as they bid him farewell for the last time.

Captain Stafford also returned to England on the flyboat with Governor White. The colonists were left with twenty longboats and two small ships, which was more than enough to transport the lot of them from the island to the mainland or another island. When last seen, the colony was trading with the Croatoan and at war with the mainland Indians. Manteo, a Native Croatoan, was still with them and a friend and ally. Imagine being a colonist. You are in a strange land thousands of miles from home. One of your own has been shot sixteen times with arrows and had his brains knocked out by Indians from the mainland. The fifteen soldiers from the year before are missing, but you find the skeleton of one of them and a report of another killed and the rest chased off by Indians from the mainland. This report is given to you by a friendly tribe, the Croatoan, as they host you to a feast. You ask them to negotiate peace with the mainland tribe (Secotan), and they agree to do so. After not hearing any word on how negotiations are going, you travel to the closest Secotan town (Dasamonquepeu) and find the Croatoan there raiding the fields. Their chief, Menatonan, was an enemy of the former Secotan chief whom English soldiers—along with Manteo and his friends—ambushed and murdered the year before. Menatonan, his wife and baby travel with you to Roanoke and witness the baptism of Manteo, who is also Croatoan. The governor instructs you to carve out the name of the place you relocate to, and you do so. You leave the word *Croatoan* on a palisade you built to protect yourself from the Secotan. These are the facts, and armed with the facts, it is no wonder why Governor John White had no doubt in his mind where the colony had relocated. The mystery of the Lost Colony was created in 1937 with the *Lost Colony* play, which ignores these facts. A more accurate description of the colony would be the abandoned colony.

Chapter 6

JOHN WHITE'S RETURN VOYAGE

1590

U nfortunately for the 1587 colony, they were abandoned for three years without resupply. It was not for a lack of effort that John White did not return sooner.

In 1588, he made an attempt to return to the colony, but all English ships were held close to Mother England by the queen for an all-out battle with the Spanish Armada. The former Portuguese pirate Simon Fernando, who had refused to take the colony to Chesapeake, made a stand against the Spanish Armada in England's largest warship, called *Triumph*. Francis Drake, who had rescued the 1585 group led by Ralph Lane, led the attack against the Spanish Armada and added to his fame to become an English hero. A lot of people know about the English defeat of the Spanish Armada, but what they do not know is that this was followed up by an attempt to invade Spain that saw the English fleet soundly defeated by a combination of Spanish and Portuguese troops. Had the war ended in 1588, it would have been easy to send a small fleet of English ships to relieve the colony. The war would continue until 1603, when Queen Elizabeth died. John White was still determined to find a way to get back to the colony, his daughter and granddaughter.

In 1589, White made another attempt to reach the colony, but the ship only made it a few miles from England before it was ambushed by the French. The French overtook them by surprise, and White was hurt in the battle. He was stabbed in the head with a pike and shot in the buttocks. Ultimately, the English defeated the French in this fight, but the English had so many wounded in that scrap with the French that they returned to England rather than continue the trip. White reported, "I myself was wounded twice in the head, once with a sword and another time with a pike, and hurt also in the side of the buttocks with a shot."

Despite his injuries, White did not give up on the colony. He recovered and tirelessly looked for a way to get back. The queen was still at war with Spain and preoccupied, but White found another way to get to the New World. The following spring, John's old friend Captain Spicer was leading a raid into the Spanish-held Caribbean and agreed to take White and stop by to check on the colony on the return voyage to England. So, the third time was a charm! In the spring of 1590, John White was finally heading back to see his daughter and granddaughter after three long years of separation.

The 1590 journey spent an enormous amount of time pillaging the Spanish on the way over. They attacked merchant ships at sea and raided Spanish-held islands even more so than Grenville had in 1585. They even happened to run into Ralph Lane in the Caribbean, who had a frigate and was also attacking the Spanish. The war with Spain was still in full swing.

When John White finally made it back to where he had left the colony, it was a rainy summer night. They passed by the island of Croatoan at night and anchored a few miles from shore during the hard rain. In the morning, the rain stopped and the ships began to sail north to Roanoke. They saw a column of black smoke coming from Kendrick's Mount, a signal the Natives often gave when they wanted to trade with the English. Right after they spotted the black smoke, a second column of smoke appeared on Roanoke Island, where Governor White had left the colonists three years prior. White believed this column of smoke to be a sign from his colonists and was eager to get back to his family, so he made the decision to go straight to Roanoke.

On the first attempt to sail through the inlet to Roanoke (near what we now call Oregon Inlet), they hit very rough water, and seven Englishmen drowned, including Captain Spicer. This event so disheartened the crew that White said many of the men argued to go home. It took hours of arguing before some of the men agreed to go with White and attempt to cross the inlet again.

It was almost dark when nineteen men, including John White, made another attempt to cross the inlet in two longboats. The waves had calmed down some, and both boats made it into the much calmer sound. By the time they reached Roanoke, it was almost pitch dark. White and his men played trumpets and drums and sang familiar English songs as they sailed by the dark island made black by the sun setting behind it. No one answered the music. Occasionally, they fired a shot into the air, hoping for some reply. They received none.

They waited until morning to go ashore on the northeast end of the island. They walked by the area where they had seen the column of smoke. It was a burned-out stump with footprints from at least two Natives around it. They then went through the woods to the west side of the island, looking toward Dasamonquepeu (Mann's Harbor), and from there returned back to the east side by walking along the shore around the northern tip of the island. They continued to walk south toward the settlement, and about a quarter of a mile north of the settlement, a large tree was found with the letters **CRO** carved on it. John White, in his own words, states that he took this to mean that the colonists must have gone to Croatoan.

They continued south along the eastern side of Roanoke Island toward the settlement site. Once they reached the site, they saw where the colonists had constructed a palisade around it. All of the houses had been carefully taken down and removed, and only some heavy iron bars, saker shot, some lead and a few tools were left behind. Saker shot is cannonballs for a saker cannon, which is a mid-sized cannon. The houses were held together by joints and wooden pegs. A simple mallet could take the frames apart, and the walls were just branches woven like a basket and covered with a mud/clay mixture. The longest process in constructing these types of houses is hewing the trees into square beams, a very laborious process; therefore, the houses being taken down is not surprising because it was easier to take them down and transport them than it was to rebuild. It also demonstrates that the colonists did not leave in haste. They had plenty of time to pack up.

At the entrance of the palisade on the right-hand side, there was a large tree as a part of the palisade. On the tree at eye level, the word *CROATOAN* was carved in all capital letters on an area of the tree with all the bark peeled off. There was no cross above or below the word. The colonists had done exactly what John White had instructed them to do when he had last seen them: they had carved the name of the place where they relocated. The colony had the time to take down their homes carefully and had time to peel off the bark of the tree and carefully carve the name *CROATOAN* in all capital letters.

Here is a direct quote from John White:

> *We passed toward the place where they were left in sundry houses, but we found the houses taken down, and the place very strongly enclosed with a high palisade of great trees, with cortynes and flankers very fort-like, and*

> *one of the chief trees or posts at the right side of the entrance had the bark taken off, and 5 foot from the ground in fair capital letters was graven CROATOAN without any cross or sign of distress; this done, we entered into the palisade, where we found many bars of Iron, two pigs of lead, four iron fowlers, Iron sacker-shot, and such like heavy things, thrown here and there, almost overgrown with grass and weeds.*

The relationships the English had with the two tribes in the area (Secotan and Croatoan) cannot be overlooked when discussing the fate of the lost colony. The colonists came to live with the Croatoan, their friends, just as they indicated with the only clue they gave as to their whereabouts, the message CROATOAN carved on the entrance of the palisade.

After finding this message from the 1587 colony, John White and his crew agreed that the next morning they would go to the island of Croatoan to relieve the settlers. In White's own words, "The next morning it was agreed by the Captain and myself, with the master and others, to weigh anchor, and go for the place at Croatoan, where our planters were."

Before White left Roanoke Island, he went to a ditch where he had buried a chest full of his armor and many books and things, only to find it had all been dug up and vandalized. White believed the Natives from Dasamonquepeu must have done it the second after they saw the colony depart for Croatoan. In this direct quote from White, he clearly indicates that the Natives of Dasamonquepeu were their enemies and must have been the ones to vandalize his things:

> *Presently Captain Cooke and I went to the place, which was in the end of an old trench, made two years past by Captain Amadas: where we found five Chests, that had been carefully hidden of the Planters, and of the same chests three were my own, and about the place many of my things spoiled and broken, and my books torn from the covers, the frames of some of my pictures and maps rotten and spoiled with rain, and my armor almost eaten through with rust; this could be no other but the deed of the Savages our enemies at Dasamonquepeu, who had watched the departure of our men to Croatoan; and as soon as they were departed, digged up every place where they suspected anything to be buried.*

The next day, the ships set sail for Croatoan. It was only fifty miles south from Roanoke Island along the "main." (The English in the sixteenth century used the word "main" to mean coastline. For example, the Spanish main was the coast of Spain. The English on the Elizabethan voyage to the Outer Banks constantly talked about sailing along the main looking for an inlet or breach to cross into the sound. Some people today confuse the word main to mean mainland, which was also true.) Unfortunately, as soon as the 1590 group set sail from Roanoke to Croatoan, they hit very bad weather. The wind was out of the northwest and blew them twenty-three miles out to sea and tore off all but one anchor. The crew had had enough and refused to turn back for Croatoan. After Captain Spicer drowned, the crew nearly turned back without having even set foot on Roanoke Island. It was only with great pressure that White was able to get some men to try to cross the inlet with him to Roanoke. There may have been a mutiny if White had pushed them to return again. Luck was not on their side. Even on the return trip home, the ship ended up wrecking at Ireland.

John White died three years later in 1593. He never saw his daughter or granddaughter again. In his last letter to Queen Elizabeth's court historian Richard Hakluyt, he said, "I greatly joyed that I had found a certain token of their safe being at Croatoan, which is the place where Manteo was born and the savages of that island our friends."

Chapter 7

LATER ATTEMPTS

The Search (or Lack Thereof) for the Colonists

I n 1602, Sir Walter Raleigh sent Samuel Mace to the New World to search for the whereabouts of the colonists left there in 1587. Mace ended up going to the Cape Fear area and collecting loads of sassafras to bring back to England, but he never made any attempt to find the colonists and never even went to Croatoan or Roanoke. He reported back to Raleigh that the weather conditions were too rough for him to go to either location.

In 1603, Sir Walter Raleigh sent out another expedition trying to find the colonists. This time, he sent both Samuel Mace and Bartholomew Gilbert to the Chesapeake area, thinking maybe they went there since that was where they originally intended to go. Gilbert was killed by Natives near the Chesapeake Bay, and the survivors reported back that they found no evidence that the colony had relocated to Chesapeake or in the woods west of there. The Spanish, having been told by a defecting colonist that the English colony was headed to Roanoke and then the Chesapeake Bay, sent a ship ordered by the governor of Florida to search the Chesapeake Bay in 1588. This ship was commanded by Vicente Gonzalez, who had been to the Chesapeake Bay before in 1570. The Spanish found no sign or word of the colony and did a very thorough search that extended from the Chesapeake Bay all the way north to the Susquehanna River. They also managed to infuriate the Indians of that region. On their way back from Chesapeake, they pulled into Port Fernando, which is Bodie (pronounce *body*) Island today and is one mile east of Roanoke Island. Here they did find a few clues. They found a slipway for small boats and two barrels buried in the sand to collect fresh water. Surprisingly and luckily for the English colony, they investigated no further. This bit of information tells us the colony did not stay very long on Roanoke Island.

The defecting colonist who told the Spanish where the English colony was headed fled the English in the Caribbean before they reached North Carolina in 1587. Therefore, he had no way of knowing the colony was never taken to the Chesapeake. He also knew nothing of the murder of George Howe, the decision to go to Croatoan, the birth of Virginia Dare or anything else that happened once the colony arrived in 1587.

While Mace and Gilbert were on their journey to search for the colony, Queen Elizabeth died and King James I took power. King James almost immediately had Sir Walter Raleigh imprisoned in the Tower of London. Raleigh was eventually beheaded in October 1618.

Many people ask, "Why didn't the Jamestown colonists hear anything about the colony?" or "Why didn't the Jamestown colonists look for the colony?" There are actually answers to both of these questions.

First, the colonists of Jamestown did hear about the Roanoke colonists. In December 1607, Chief Powhatan's brother Opechancanough told the Jamestown explorers that the colonists of 1587 were living with the Natives at Ocanahonan, where "people wear English clothing" and there is "a great turning of saltwater," according to Helen Rountree's *Powhatan Indians of Virginia*.

Diamond Shoals is a famous ship hazard that runs perpendicular to Croatoan/Hatteras where two major ocean currents collide, creating a great turning of salt water for twelve to fourteen miles 365 days a year. It makes sense that Ocanahonan [Oh-cah-nah-hoe-nan] refers to Croatoan (which is the English mispronunciation of *kurawoten*). *Ku-rah-woe-tain* is the Algonquian word for "council town." There are many Algonquian words that the Jamestown explorers wrote down that are slightly different than the words the Elizabethans had already recorded in the 1500s. We do not know if this is due to subtle differences between how the Powhatan tribes pronounced things versus how the North Carolina tribes did or if it is just a difference in what the English thought they heard. It could also be a combination of both factors. Regardless of where Ocanahonan is/was, the English at Jamestown made no attempt to find it.

So why didn't they attempt to find their brethren?

In 1607, it had been twenty years since the colonists were last seen. To the English at this time, they were hearing how the English and Natives were living together as one and had assimilated into an interracial culture. To them, it was a disgrace. They were appalled and did not want to see it or speak of it. Unfortunately, at that time in history, Natives were seen as less human, less civilized, to the Europeans. Even Thomas Harriot and John White referred to them as "savages." It was racism and egocentrism, and unfortunately, it was a sentiment that would persist all the way to the modern day for many, as there are still many who are loath or hesitant to admit the blaring truth: that the colonists assimilated into the Native culture and became one family. They were one of the earliest examples of the American melting pot.

⁓⧔⧕⁓

WE HEAR NOTHING MORE of the colonists until 1701, when the explorer John Lawson published his book *A New Voyage to Carolina*. Lawson was hired by the Lords Proprietors, a group of wealthy Englishmen appointed by the Crown to govern the settlement of Carolina, to survey all the Native tribes in Carolina and write up his findings. North and South Carolina at that time were still one colony simply called Carolina.

What Lawson found when he visited Hatteras Island (Croatoan) was evidence of the colony. He found gray-eyed Indians wearing English-style clothes who said they had white ancestors who could read out of a book, and they even mentioned Sir Walter Raleigh by name.

Here are some quotes from Lawson talking about the Hatteras tribe:

> *Hatteras tribe: These tell us, that several of their Ancestors were white People, and could talk in a Book, as we do; the Truth of which is confirmed by gray Eyes being found frequently amongst these Indians, and no others. They value themselves extremely for their Affinity to the English, and are ready to do them all friendly Offices.*
>
> *I cannot forbear inserting here, a pleasant Story that passes for an uncontested Truth amongst the Inhabitants of this Place; which is, that the Ship which brought the first Colonies, does often appear amongst them, under Sail, in a gallant Posture, which they call Sir Walter Raleigh's Ship; And the truth of this has been affirmed to me, by Men of the best Credit in the Country.*
>
> *Hatteras Indians: these are them that wear English dress.*

Lawson's report of an Indian/European mixed race being found on Hatteras Island was still appalling to Europeans even in the early 1700s. Lawson's exact words are as follows:

> *It is probable, that this Settlement miscarried for want of timely Supplies from England; or thro' the Treachery of the Natives, for we may reasonably suppose that the English were forced to cohabit with them, for Relief and Conversation; and that in process of Time, they conformed themselves to the Manners of their Indian Relations. And thus we see, how apt Human Nature is to degenerate.*

It is important to note at this point that Lawson, who was somewhat horrified by finding that the English had "degenerated" and assimilated with the Natives, who were still considered less-than their European counterparts, still admitted that the 1587 colonists' descendants had been found. There is no mystery at this point. Unlike the Jamestown colonists in the early 1600s, Lawson was at least willing to admit that the colonists had assimilated, but he could not hide his overt racism and egocentrism in his own culture and race.

In 1710, a missionary by the name of Reverend John Irmstone visited Hatteras Island. Irmstone was a missionary of the Society for the Propagation of the Gospel in Foreign Parts, which was established in 1701 by the Church of England. Reverend Irmstone wrote in a letter to his superiors about people from Hatteras who came to get baptized. He explicitly stated that "these persons are half Indian and half English" and were "an offense to my own." Even a claimed Godly man of the time was racist and looked down on these assimilated peoples. He further stated in horrific fashion that he "gravely doubts the Kingdom of Heaven was designed to accommodate such people."

∞

This racism is a harsh reality of our history of America—and unfortunately, it is still a harsh reality in our world today. Let us not forget the Native people of America who still fight for what little land they have left of what was originally theirs and was stolen from them by European settlers.

The model for colonization that Raleigh, Harriot, White and Hakluyt envisioned of harmony with the Native peoples and mutually benefiting societies almost happened, even if only on a tiny island called Croatoan. Unfortunately, this model for settlement was abandoned, just like the 1587 colony.

Jamestown was settled by a company bent on tobacco profits. It was not interested in ethnography. Almost all images you see representing Powhatan Indians are John White's paintings of North Carolina Indians because the Jamestown lot did not bother to paint any. What resulted in the first winter at Jamestown was the death of 154 out of 214 people, due mainly to starvation. One man even ate his own wife, and many others ate leather. It is only through sheer weight and constant wave after wave of settlers that Jamestown survived.

The dismissive and racist attitude toward the Native Americans continued for centuries to come. Even in the 1800s, Natives in California had bounties placed on them. Indians were hunted like animals, and forty pounds sterling was rewarded for killing a man, twenty for a woman and ten for a child.

In the 1880s, U.S. Army captain Richard Henry Pratt came up with a particularly heinous idea to crush Native heritage for good that became a law called the Boarding School Act. Native American children from around the country were rounded up and taken from their parents and sent to boarding schools. They were not allowed any contact with their families. They were beaten if they spoke their Native language and given new Anglo-Saxon names. A third of these children died at the schools before the age of ten. The Boarding School Act continued into the early twentieth century. There are people still living who were sent to these schools. To document all the atrocities committed against Native peoples by the U.S. government is too depressing and monumental a task, but it is fair to say that men like Thomas Harriot were centuries ahead of their time when it came to their attitude toward Native Americans. The Elizabethan voyages to the New World are a story of what could have been if not for a storm in 1590.

So, WHERE DO WE go from here?

At this point, it should seem obvious that the colonists went to Croatoan, just as they indicated. The only question left is, what did they do after they went to Croatoan? How long did they stay there? Did they split up? Did they attempt to sail for home on a pinnace and drown? Did they live at Croatoan for a few years and then move elsewhere? What percentage of them starved or died in the first few years? Historical records cannot provide us with all the answers, so ultimately, we have to look to archaeology to help us fill in the blanks and answer these and other questions. As alluded to in the foreword, it appears they simply lived out their days on Croatoan and completely assimilated. It would take archaeology to uncover this fate.

— *Part II* —
ARCHAEOLOGY

Archaeological layers. *Author's collection.*

Chapter 8

NATIVE LIFE

It is always important to know as much as you can about the people who lived on the land you are digging and investigating through archaeology. The English people on the sixteenth-century Elizabethan voyages encountered several different tribes, but they mainly interacted with two: the Secotan and the Croatoan. The first English voyage to the New World in 1584 brought one Native male from each of these tribes back to England with them: Manteo from the Croatoan tribe and Wanchese from the Secotan tribe. These two Native men spent the winter of 1584 in England with Thomas Harriot in his home before being returned to their home the following spring. While in England, Harriot learned as much as he could from his New World guests and vice versa. Manteo actually returned to England a second time in 1586 and spent another entire winter there and then returned to Croatoan (Hatteras Island) in 1587 with the Lost Colony. By that time, Manteo had become fairly fluent in the English language and served as an interpreter between the colonists and was eventually even baptized.

POPULATION

When ethnographer Thomas Harriot visited northeastern North Carolina in 1585, most of the land was still virgin forest, marshes and flats teeming with wildlife. Native settlements were made up of small villages of a few hundred people living primarily along creeks and rivers or along the sound side of the Outer Banks. The largest town the English came across was Chowan, near modern-day Colerain, North Carolina, and it only had thirty longhouses. However, it had a population of around seven hundred people. This is because the longhouses the Native people lived in contained extended family, not just a mom, dad and kids. One longhouse often included aunts/uncles/cousins/grandparents. Some of the longhouses were sixty feet in length, and it was not uncommon for twenty to thirty people to reside in one longhouse. The longhouses were framed from saplings that were bent and tied together with cordage made from several different local plants. The sapling frames made an arch-shaped ceiling that was sometimes covered with animal skins or reeds and bark.

The exact population of Hatteras Island in the sixteenth century is unknown because no accurate census was ever recorded, but Harriot did give us a clue by mentioning how many longhouses he encountered. The largest town on the seacoast had twenty houses, and some had as few as ten or twelve. Roanoke Island, according to Arthur Barlowe, who visited there in 1584, had a total of nine houses. German engraver Theodore de Bry made a map based on a watercolor map done by John White. On White's map, he indicated Indian villages with the color red and placed red dots on the map to indicate a Native town. On Croatoan, he colored the entire island red. On the de Bry map, towns were indicated by a circle made of vertical lines like a palisade. De Bry marked three towns on Croatoan.

If Chowan had an estimated 700 people and thirty houses, then an average of 23 to 24 people lived in a longhouse, which also matches what Jamestown records say about Native dwellings. If you use 23 as the average number, it would put the largest Croatoan village, located today in Buxton, which had twenty houses—at roughly 460 people. An additional 276 people were living where Hatteras Village sits now, and if there was a third village on Hatteras Island in the sixteenth century, as indicated by the de Bry map, it would chip in another 230 people. This third village has yet to be confirmed or even investigated by archaeology, but we know where it is from accidental contact by construction workers. As it stands now, a lot of Native pottery and material have been found by Buxton locals and CAS members Davis Thatch and Scott Dawson in an area spanning a quarter of a mile that has not been tested yet by archaeologists. In any case, the third village was certainly not very large. Therefore, an educated guess based on the information available would put the total Native population

Croatoan longhouse. *Painted by William Brown.*

of Hatteras Island upon European contact in the late sixteenth century at approximately 790 to perhaps as many as 1,000 people, split between at least two and possibly three villages, all of which were on the sound side of the island. An article in the *Hatteras Monitor* discussing the work of Dr. David Phelps, who conducted several digs on Hatteras Island in the 1990s, estimated the population to be much higher at 6,000 people.

There is also at least two Mid-Woodland village sites (500 BCE–500 CE) on Hatteras Island. One is where the village of Frisco is today, and the other rests behind and underneath the high school in Buxton. The one in Frisco was investigated in 2009 and 2011 by CAS and UoB but has since been utterly destroyed by development. The one at the high school was discovered by chance in 2013 when the dig team went to the high school to demonstrate how a dig is conducted. The students were able to fit together thirteen large pieces of Native pottery that sit in a display case inside the school today.

American Indian populations across eastern North Carolina and sadly the entire East Coast were rapidly and greatly reduced by European diseases, war and intermarriage with white people. The Pamlico Indians, located about forty-five miles west of Croatoan, were nearly completely killed off in 1695 by a smallpox epidemic. By the start of the eighteenth century, when John Lawson retraced the footsteps of Harriot and the Elizabethan explorers, the Chowan and Hatteras tribes had been reduced to sixteen fighting men apiece. Fighting men represented about a fifth of the total population, meaning both of those tribes, which had numbered around seven hundred people, each had been reduced to around eighty, and the Hatteras tribe was now consolidated into a single town. Diseases had taken such a horrible toll that some of the villages were completely annihilated and had wolves chewing on unburied corpses when Lawson came across them.

LANGUAGE

The Croatoan and Secotan, while enemies with each other and completely different in their relationship with the English (Croatoan were allies, the Secotan enemies), were culturally identical. They spoke the same language and had the same diet, technologies, religious beliefs, burial practices, dress, warfare, political structure and so forth. The Croatoan and Secotan in the sixteenth century also had a lot in common with the better-known Powhatan of Virginia. All three were part of the Algonquian language family, although with different dialects. There are twenty-nine distinct dialects of Algonquian spoken from North Carolina to Canada. The Outer Banks were the extreme southern border of the language. The dialect of the Natives the English met in the 1580s is called Carolina Algonquian and was spoken by the Chowan, Croatoan, Secotan, Pamlico and others native to the tidewater area of North Carolina. An English-Carolina Algonquian word list is included at the end of this book, but it is a language that is no longer used.

NATIVE DIET

Farming was not practiced on a large scale, but the Natives did live in year-round permanent towns with large gardens. We know the people on Hatteras Island lived there year-round because of the types of shellfish found in the middens. Shellfish from all four seasons are found in abundance, mixed in with fish, deer and turtle bones. Corn (*pagatowr*) was probably the main agricultural product. Also grown were beans, squash, pumpkins, sunflowers, peas, cucumbers, gourds and tobacco. The gourds were used to carry water because they were much lighter than clay pots, which they used to boil stews and cook meats. The tobacco grown by the Natives in the sixteenth century was of a different strain than that which is grown in North Carolina today. The tobacco the Natives grew had nine times as much nicotine and was much harsher to smoke. It also had a mild hallucinogenic effect

Contrary to popular myth, Ralph Lane of the 1585 expedition was not the first person to bring tobacco to England. That honor, or perhaps dishonor, belongs to a Frenchman named Jean Nicot, who brought the tobacco from Portugal to England in 1556. Nicot is where we get the word *nicotine*.

In addition to growing food, the Natives foraged a vast variety of nuts, berries and edible roots from plants such as greenbrier, which was then

Ein höltzern Roost/darauff sie die Fische besengen. XIIII.

Ann sie eine grosse menge Fische haben gefangen/begeben sie sich auff einen dar zu verordneten Platz/welcher die Speiß zu bereiten bequeme ist/daselbst stecken sie vier Gabeln auff einem vierecketen Platz in die Erden hinein/auff diese legen sie vier Höltzer/und auff dieselbigen andere zwerchsweise/also/daß es einem Roost/der da hoch gnugsam sey/gleichförmig werde. Wann sie die Fische auff den Roost gelegt/machen sie ein Fewer darunter/doch nicht nach der weise der Völcker von Florida/welche die Fisch allein besengen/und im Rauch außtrücknen/die sie den gantzen Winter über behalten. Diese Völcker aber braten alles/verzehrens/und behalten nichts in vorraht/darnach/wann sie dessen dörfftig sind/braten oder sieden sie frische/wie wir hernach sehen werden. Wann aber der Roost so groß nicht ist/daß die Fisch alle möchten darauff gelegt werden/stecken sie kleine steckkein am Fewer in die Erden/und hencken die übrigen Fische durch die Ohren auff/und braten sie vollends so lang es gnug sey. Sie sehen aber mit fleiß zu/daß sie nicht verbrennt werden. Wann die ersten gebraten sind/legen sie andere/so sie frisch herzu gebracht/auff den Roost. Und also widerholen sie diß braten so lange/biß sie der Speise gnugsam zu haben vermeynen.

How the natives cooked fish. *Library of Congress.*

processed into bread. Many roots were also used to make dyes, medicines and sweeteners such as sassafras. Plants were also used to make rope and baskets, repel insects or even purge the body. For example, jimson weed or morning glory seeds were used to cure burns and inflammations.

Yaupon leaves were used to make what the Europeans labeled the "black drink." This drink was used in a ceremony or holiday that was meant to be a day of forgiveness toward everyone in the tribe, sometimes called the green corn ceremony. It was held in late summer when the first harvest of corn was ready. It was a day to start anew. The black drink was made from the leaves of the yaupon bush that were not roasted but rather chopped up raw and mixed with hot water. It caused whoever drank it to vomit violently and charged them with a huge caffeine buzz. The vomiting was a physical symbol of getting everything bad out of the body so that everyone could start over with a clean slate. Yaupon also contains more caffeine than coffee and, if the leaves are roasted before being processed into tea, makes a fine drink that is still consumed on Hatteras Island today, even at church. In fact, yaupon production and sale to the mainland remained a part of Hatteras Island culture well into the early twentieth century. The phrase "kinnakeeter yaupon eater" comes from the large amount of yaupon processed in the village of Kinnakeet on Hatteras Island, and saying said phrase in Kinnakeet today is a good way to get beat up.

Hunting and fishing were a huge part of the diet and everyday life of the Native Croatoan. The main animal hunted was deer. Not only could the animal provide a lot of meat but also clothing. The same was true for black bear, which were/are numerous on the North Carolina mainland. The hamstrings of the deer were used for the strings of bows, and the antlers were used for a variety of tools and even as pipe bowls. Bows and arrows were the main weapons used to hunt deer, although spears were also used.

Fishing was done by nets, spears and traps. Fish, crabs, turtles and shellfish were eaten in great abundance by the Croatoan. Lawson describes a creative way the Natives had for catching crabs and other shellfish where they halfway cooked some venison and then cut it into strips that then had a sharp reed stuck through them. They took the baited reeds and stuck the sharp end of the reed into the bottom of the water and waited. Every now and then, they would check the baited reeds and take off the shellfish, then repeat the process. The larger fish they caught from the ocean were dried and smoked on hurdles made of canes in the shape of a gridiron; thus, the meat could be stored.

The most effective form of fishing was the weir net system. It is from this system that we get pound netting designs today. Fish will instinctively

Croatoan weir nets. *Painted by William Brown.*

swim toward deeper water when they encounter a barrier. The Natives built fences made from river cane that were perpendicular to sandbars or shore and led fish into deeper water but also into a series of spade-shaped rooms that trapped the fish without causing them any harm. This method allowed the fishermen to release any fish they did not wish to eat. The Natives had a great respect for nature. It was a custom not to eat the first fish caught in a weir. Weirs were also blessed at the end of construction; a bit of tobacco was sprinkled into the air and the water around the weir.

TRANSPORTATION

The only forms of transportation the Natives had were by foot or canoe. Horses did not arrive until Europeans brought them over. In fact, it is possible that the wild ponies on Ocracoke Island today are descendants of Richard Grenville's 1585 shipwreck of the *Tiger*, which had horses released from it in an effort to get off the bar. Due to the transportation limits, chiefdoms or nations did not stretch across vast areas of land. Anything over eighty miles would be considered a huge chiefdom. It is hard to communicate with, much less rule over, people who are more than two days' travel away. Chiefdoms were made up of towns and villages that had *weroances*, which were like mayors. The chiefdom would have one paramount chief who had the final say on large issues such as war. Day-to-day issues of a town or village were handled by weroances, which in turn had councils made up of members of their town. Both men and women could be weroances, and status was indicated by wearing copper.

RELIGION

According to Thomas Harriot, the Natives of the Outer Banks and adjacent mainland believed in many gods but had only one chief god that has existed forever and created the other gods to help manage the universe. They said the Earth and creatures on it were made from the water by the gods and also believed in an afterlife. If you were good on Earth, you went to heaven, and if not, you went to a place called Popogusso, which was a pit of darkness and great suffering located here on Earth where the sun sets.

A morgue called a *machucomick* that housed the dead. An idol made of clay sits at the bottom with a shell and copper necklace. *Library of Congress.*

They had temples called *machucomicks* where the dead were stored for a time before being buried, much like a morgue. In the machucomick, idols of an ancestral god called Kewas were placed by the bodies. Kewas looked like a human and was always in a squatting or kneeling position. All of the gods were believed to be of human form. These idols were made of clay and wood; painted black, red and white; and then adorned with shell and copper necklaces.

Copper was very highly valued by the Natives and a symbol of power and prestige. The political leaders of the tribes wore copper. There is no source for copper on the coast of North Carolina, so all the copper was imported from tribes much farther inland. They would also pan for copper in the rivers and then melt it down in clay pots. The English would take advantage of the high value of copper in the New World and trade English copper for a variety of goods, mainly leather from deer hides. Leather merchants were major investors in the second English voyage to the New World. Twenty-three years after the English landed in North Carolina, the Jamestown colony was founded in Virginia and barrels of copper were brought over by the English to use as trade items.

PETS

In Walt Disney's *Pocahontas*, there are many things completely made up, as one would expect in a cartoon movie. In the movie, Pocahontas has a pet raccoon. There is no evidence that Pocahontas had a pet raccoon, but it is true that the Natives did sometimes raise raccoons as pets and they were quite tame. I have known a few people in Tennessee as well as North Carolina who had tame raccoons as pets, which validates what

Lawson reported. The people on the coast of North Carolina also had dogs, which the English described as "wolfish." The type of dog has never been identified, and it is possible they may have been coyotes, since no species of dog has yet been identified as indigenous to North Carolina. Some coyote teeth have been found in Croatoan middens, but since the animal might also have been eaten, it cannot be confirmed that they were raised as pets.

GENDER ROLES

The Natives had marriages and divorces, but only a female could divorce the man; the man could not divorce the female. Lineage, unlike in Europe, was through the female side of the family. To the European observer, gender roles favored the men though because women did all the farming, childcare, cooking and basically everything aside from hunting, fishing and building houses. To Europeans, hunting and fishing were viewed more as sport, things done in leisure time rather than daily work.

The men were a warrior class of people who went through an initiation process as boys into accepted manhood. In Virginia, the initiation process was called *huskanaw*. The huskanaw was a tribe-wide event where all boys thought to be ready for the initiation into manhood (usually around fifteen years of age) were gathered together for the process, which would take months. Some Europeans mistook the huskanaw for child sacrifice. It was a brutal process. First there was a dance. There were two rings of people, one ring inside the other, with one dancing around the center in a clockwise fashion and the other ring dancing counterclockwise. In the middle were people with black horns. There was also a great feast that lasted two or three hours. The boys in the huskanaw had to endure being beaten with reeds and were given a hallucinogenic drink and taken to the wilderness for weeks or even months at a time. They went so mad from the hallucinogenic drink and beatings that they had to be put in cages made of latticework in the shape of a cone. What exactly happened in the wilderness is a mystery, but when they returned—and not all did— they were considered men and were publicly given a new name by their weroances. It took weeks to be gradually brought off the drugs.

Toughness was an important virtue. It was custom of many tribes from the Carolinas to the Great Lakes to torture war prisoners by cutting and burning them. The captives were expected not to cry out and to die with honor. Without currency or wages, the only way to acquire wealth was by being a great hunter or fisherman. Meat and skins made a man a good provider; only copper, shell beads, tobacco and a few other commodities made up the short list of coveted material items. Thus, a man was a hunter/warrior.

Dancing

Dances were an intricate part of Native society and played a major role in the culture. Dancing was practiced daily and done in large groups. Rather than men and women pairing off in couples and dancing to music, an entire tribe would dance all together on a daily basis. There were all sorts of dances—a victory dance, a war dance, a welcome dance, the dance that set up the huskanaw, dances to celebrate harvest time as well as nightly social dances. The music besides singing was mostly rattles made of gourds. Skins stretched over hollow pieces of wood made fine drums, and reed flutes were used. Usually a dance went around something—a fire, group of people or such thing. The Elizabethans described several dances, and John White painted a few images of what he observed that show clearly the gourd rattles.

Technology

The lack of iron was probably the greatest difference between Natives and Europeans. Not having iron tools affects the ability to manipulate wood, as in the building of houses, canoes or anything that involves cutting wood. The clearing of fields for farming and plowing was also affected by the lack of access to iron. There is a reason man's progress is lumped into categories such as the stone age, the bronze age and the iron age. The types of metals a society has access to affect so many facets of life. Iron is what allowed Europeans to have guns, cannons, armor, large farms and houses and ships. There is no doubt the Natives recognized the value of iron because it was iron tools more than anything else that they traded their skins, pearls and tobacco to get.

Natives at a campfire with rattles made of gourds. *Library of Congress.*

Yet despite having no iron prior to European contact, the Natives lived long, healthy lives, getting everything they needed from the land where they lived, and still had enough time for games, sports, dancing and leisure. They did not have to spend their lives working to pay someone else for land or a house they lived in. There was no such thing as debt, a mortgage or even rent. There was no such thing as disease. People worked together to provide necessities and spent the rest of their time doing whatever they wanted. No one owned the land. In Native society, the gap between the haves and the have-nots was very narrow in comparison to Europeans, where some lived in castles with servants and an abundance of material wealth while others were homeless beggars.

Lintrium conficiendorum ratio. XII.

IEA est in VIRGINIA cymbas fabricandi ratio: nam, cum ferreis instrumentis aut aliis nostris similibus careant, eas tamen pa are ne-runt nostris non minus commodas ad nauigandum quo lubet per flumi-na et adpiscandum. Primum arbore aliqua crassa et alta delecta, pro cymba parate volunt magnitudine, ignem circa eius radices summa tellure in ambitu struunt ex arborum musco bene resiccato, et ligni assulis paulatim ignem excitantes, ne flamma altius ascendat, et arboris longitudinem minuat. Pane adusta et ruinam minante arbo-re, nouum suscitant ignem, quem flagrare sinunt, donec arbor sponte cadat. Adustis deinde arbo-ris fastigio et ramis, vt truncus iustam longitudinem retineat, lignis transuersis supra furcas po-sitis imponunt, ea altitudine vt commode laborare possint, tunc cortice conchis quibusdam adem-pto, integriorem trunci partem pro cymba inferiore parte seruant, in altera parte ignem secundum trunci longitudinem struunt, praterquam extremis, quod satis adustum illic videtur, restincto igne conchis scabunt, et nouo suscitato igne denuo adurunt, atque ita deinceps pergunt, subinde vren-tes et scabentes, donec cymba necessarium alueum nacta sit. Sic Domini spiritus rudibus homini-bus sug gerit rationem, qua res in suum vsum necessarias conficere queant.

B 4

How Natives built canoes. The artist, Theodore de Bry, added the idea of having the trees lifted off the ground. In reality, they were on the ground and the sides were packed with mud. This way, when they burned the top of the tree it would not burn the sides. Shells, bones and antlers were used to hollow out the trees. *Library of Congress.*

Native people ate and danced together as a tribe and every morning would bathe and thank the sun and the Earth for providing what they needed. They had respect for all plants and animals and a policy not to waste any part of an animal that they killed to eat. Nature was something to respect and live in harmony with rather than something to conquer. The idea that American Indians were primitive in comparison to their European counterparts is a narrow-minded one that does not appreciate the complexity of the culture.

Chapter 9

INTRODUCTION TO ARCHAEOLOGY

L et's talk about the context of layers. How do we date the layers of soil or stratigraphy? Dating of layers often occurs by the pottery, both Native and European pottery sherds/shards. Both Native and European pottery have a specific dating system. Pottery is most often used because it tends to be the most abundant artifact in the layer. Pipes and glass bottles can also be used to date the layer of soil, as they also have a well-defined dating system called a typology.

What about coins? It is wonderful when the layer just so happens to have a coin with a date on it; however, all it really tells you is that the layer can be no older than that date. For example, if you are digging a layer and out pops a coin with the date 1642, what that tells you is that the layer can't possibly be from 1620, but it can be any time after 1642. Perhaps it could be 1642, the year of the mint, *or* it could be any time after 1642. Look in your pocket or purse. You have coins of many different years, but none will have future years on them. So you can't have a layer of time in the Earth's soil with a future coin in it either, but someone could have had a coin from a previous decade or decades in their pocket or purse and been walking around with it and dropped it. So if you find a coin in a layer that is a coin minted 1642, then perhaps the layer is at the oldest 1642, but it is more accurate to say the layer is the mid-1600s or mid-seventeenth century.

In archaeology, we look at where we found the artifact—what layer, what context. What level, what stratum the artifact was found in matters.

For decades if not centuries, the local and Native people of Hatteras Island have been unearthing artifacts while building homes or digging forts in the woods while at play. There are many such stories as these, but a few are quite noteworthy and deserve being shared, despite being out of context.

In the 1920s, my great-grandfather Eustes White found an intact Spanish olive jar that stands a foot tall and still remains in one of my family member's homes today. It was examined by Professor Mark Horton and then returned to my family member. According to Dr. Horton, what Eustes found is probably the oldest intact European ceramic ever found in North Carolina. In the early part of the twentieth century, Buxton woods contained several trash dumps that were huge holes dug out and filled with trash. Eustes found this jug when his dog uncovered part of it while digging a hole in one of these locations in the woods. This jug was near one of the dumps, but no one remembers precisely where because the holes have been filled in since then. It appears to be a Spanish olive jar from the sixteenth century. These were commonly used by all of western Europe and the Mediterranean during that time. The jar likely contained

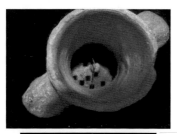

The sixteenth-century olive jar. *Author's collection.*

olive oil or wine. When looking down into the jug, one can see that there is a sort of clay screen with quarter-inch square holes in it. Whatever was once in the jug was almost certainly a liquid because nothing else would fit through the tiny screen. We know that Sir Francis Drake stole several olive jars of this type in 1585 from Spanish colonies in Florida. We also know that olive oil was needed in England to process the number-one export: wool. After Drake stole all the jars from Florida in 1585, he made his way to Croatoan, where he lost a ship from his fleet called the *Francis* to bad weather. Was this olive jar once on the *Francis*? Did it wash ashore? Did it come to Croatoan and get traded by another Elizabethan voyage? Was it from the wreck of the 1560s Spanish ship that the Croatoan told Amadas and Barlowe about? It is impossible to say because the jar was not found in context.

Another story of a local Hatteras find is just as exciting but with an unfortunate outcome. In the early 1930s, Charles "Lindy" Miller was out playing in the woods off Rocky Rollinson Road, digging around to build a fort, when he came across something quite exciting: an old sword. He also found several bones, arrowheads, buttons and a large pot, but it was the sword that really captured everyone's attention. The *Dare County Times* ran an article about the find and took Lindy's picture for the paper.

Dare County Times clipping saved by Jack Gray of Buxton. Photo of Lindy Miller after his discovery of a sword and other items in the same spot where the Croatoan village digs would occur 60 years later.

A 1937 newspaper clipping. *Author's collection.*

Buxton Boy Finds an Ancient Sword
Lindy Miller, young son of Mr. and Mrs. Cantwell Miller is the owner of an ancient sword, recently found in a hillside near Cape Hatteras. At this spot, have been found many arrowheads, bits of pottery, and other Indian relics. At one spot nearby, the finding of some brass buttons, led to the location of some Admiral's bones, and they were removed by his people, who had not known before where he was buried. The whole section is rich in historical significance, and local citizens now speculate as to what type of sword it is. Some people think it was left there during the Civil War.

Unfortunately, the State of North Carolina took an interest in this and confiscated the sword from Lindy and his family. The sword was taken to the Museum of Natural History in Raleigh to study and curate it, but it was never put on display and never returned. I called the Museum of Natural History in Raleigh myself multiple times to inquire about the sword, even quoting the *Dare County Times* article, only to be told they have no record of the sword. The furthest I ever got was that they would "check their archives and get back to me." Of course, I never heard back, so I called again after a few weeks, and they told me they had no luck finding any such sword.

⤬

THE FIRST TIME ANY real preliminary archaeological work was done on Hatteras Island was in 1938, when the National Park Service became interested in designating the island a national recreational facility. The federal government began some very surface investigations. These investigations, although limited in scope, gave some indications of the archaeological content of the region. Joffre Coe from the Laboratory of Anthropology at the University of North Carolina–Chapel Hill made some minor excavations near Buxton on Hatteras Island that basically consisted of surface survey work. He did, however, have the Cape Creek area designated as significant enough of a midden to receive the Smithsonian designation 31DR1, which means it is an archaeological area of interest.

Between 1947 and 1953, archaeologist J.C. Harrington conducted archaeological excavations on Roanoke Island. While he was conducting his work on Roanoke, he was given a casting counter, or Nuremberg token, from a resident of Hatteras Island by the name of Tandy. A casting counter looks like a coin and is made of copper and zinc. They were used on a counting board similar to an abacus to count inventory on ships. Tandy reportedly found the token on Hatteras Island, and this casting counter was an exact match of a casting counter found twenty years later on Roanoke Island that was believed to be from the sixteenth century, likely from the Roanoke voyages. Two more casting counters were also found on Roanoke but were slightly different. Harrington never conducted any excavations on Hatteras; however, he kept Tandy's Nuremberg token for study.

∽∞⌒

IN 1954 AND 1955, the Office of Naval Research sponsored an extensive archaeological survey of the northeastern coastal region of North Carolina from Currituck Sound to the Neuse River. This research, under the direction of William Haag, was carried out as part of a program to develop the Cape Hatteras National Seashore Park. Haag was charged with finding sites that depicted the ancient history of the region; he also was directed to find evidence of the whereabouts of members of the Lost Colony after they abandoned Fort Raleigh. The latter goal dictated that Haag's survey focus on the Cape Hatteras area, where many believed the English settlers moved after leaving Roanoke Island. Haag recorded a total of sixty-nine sites, most of which were located on Hatteras Island and along the north bank of the mouth of the Pamlico River. Like most archaeological surveys along the coast, pottery sherds constituted the main body of Haag's data. Although he saw considerable variability in the way vessel surfaces were treated, he regarded temper as the most "culturally important" attribute. Pottery thought to be the earliest contained a mixture of sand and grit temper, whereas later ceramics were shell tempered.

Basically, Haag was sent to Hatteras to find evidence of the Lost Colony since they were believed to have gone there from Roanoke based on the fact that the colony carved the old name of Hatteras Island, Croatoan, into a tree. Haag found evidence of where the Croatoan village was, yet nothing was done.

In 1974, teenagers playing near a construction site in Hatteras Village ran into a pile of "old bones" where a new home was being built. They contacted the appropriate channels, and Dr. David Phelps, archaeologist from East Carolina University (ECU) in Greenville, North Carolina, came to Hatteras Village and excavated a large ossuary containing human remains. I asked him about the remains by e-mail, and he responded that they came from at least 110 different skeletons of all ages and both genders. The remains were radiocarbon dated to 1395 CE. Radiocarbon dating has a variance of plus or minus 200 years.

I also talked to some of the people who made the initial discovery, all adults now, and they said the skeletons were in rows with the skulls in two rows, the long bones stacked together in front of the skulls and the other bones in a pile next to the long bones. So there was an order to the burial, and the bones were buried long after the individuals had died. It was custom for the Indians in the area to keep the dead in a morgue called a *machucomick* and then bury all who died that year at once during the solstice after polishing the bones with bear grease.

In 1983, Dr. Phelps returned to Hatteras Island, working under the sponsorship of America's Four Hundredth Anniversary Committee, and performed the first actual archaeological test "excavation" in the Buxton area (31DR1). His research concluded that the buried stratum that contained the evidence of Croatoan Village was rich and intact.

In 1993, Hurricane Emily hit Hatteras Island and uncovered a massive amount of archaeology on the sound side of Buxton in the area of 31DR1. Local Hatteras Island residents Xander Brody, Fred Willard and Barbara Midgette discovered a gold mine of artifacts on the sound side in Buxton after the storm. "Enough to fill the back of a pickup truck," said Willard. Willard contacted Dr. Phelps at ECU in hopes of getting him to come and excavate the area.

Dr. Phelps returned to Hatteras to survey the area a few times, and then in 1998, he conducted a full-scale archaeological excavation in conjunction with the Lost Colony Center for Science and Research, founded by Fred Willard. Phelps and Willard worked together with ECU and the local community to uncover archaeology in the area of 31DR1. During the Phelps excavations, lots of Native and European artifacts were found, such as native pottery, whelk shell tools/hoes, Native and European pipes, lead shot and nails, copper, glass beads, gun flints, glass bottles and fragments, bricks, pigs' teeth and many other significant finds. However, the two most significant finds were the famous gunlock and Kendall ring.

The gunlock is a late sixteenth-century snaphaunce that may have arrived in Buxton during one of the sixteenth-century Elizabethan voyages. The gunlock is identical to one in a museum in England that was made in 1583. It was found in a seventeenth-century stratus layer, which means that someone held on to it for a generation or so before discarding it.

The Kendall ring was actually dug up by local Hatteras islander Chris Ballance, who was volunteering with the ECU crew. The ring was found in the general debris around an Indian workshop or trading center. It was originally believed to be gold, but then in 2018, XRF technology found it to be made of bronze. It has a prancing lion engraved on it and was once believed to have belonged to Master Kendall, a member of the 1585–86 expedition. Master Kendall was sent to Croatoan by Ralph Lane to live with the tribe during the 1585–86 expedition, and it may have been traded during his time there. As it turns out, a prancing lion is a very common seal and could have belonged to a number of people from the 1587 or 1585 colonists. The ring was found in a seventeenth-century stratum, so it was clearly held on to for a generation before being lost or discarded.

Another major outcome from Phelps's dig in 1998 was the confirmation of the long-held belief that the 31DR1 area was and is the capital town of Croatoan.

Unfortunately, all of the artifacts from Phelps's digs left the island and have not returned. They are all currently stored at East Carolina University and are still being processed, catalogued and curated, and nothing is on display. Even the ring and gunlock cannot be seen unless by special permission, and even then only by a select few. According to the property owner where the ring and gunlock were found, some of the artifacts found during these digs by Phelps have gone missing completely after being sent out for special testing.

In 2007, I self-published a book called *Croatoan: Birthplace of America* through Times Printing in Manteo, North Carolina, about the Lost Colony of 1587. Professor and archaeologist Mark Horton with the University of Bristol in England heard about me and the book while doing some work for Festival

Park in Manteo. He decided he needed to come take a look at Hatteras for the missing colonists of 1587 from his homeland. I got him a place to stay and permission from property owners to dig on their land.

This leads us to the Croatoan Archaeological Society–University of Bristol (CAS/UoB) Archaeological Project, which spanned from 2009 to 2018. Appropriately titled the Croatoan Archaeological Project, the CAP unearthed an enormous amount of knowledge on the Native Americans of Hatteras Island and the Native-European contact period.

We have evidence of people on Hatteras Island over thirteen thousand years ago. The oldest documented artifact found on Hatteras Island came out of the earth in Buxton and is a Cumberland point that dates back to 11,000 BCE, or thirteen thousand years ago. The spearhead in the following photo is more than twice the age of the pyramids of Giza in Egypt! This spearhead was found by a Buxton local when a massive oak tree blew over and the roots were dug out to avoid a hazard. It was measured, drawn and photographed by CAS-UoB in 2010 and then returned to its owner.

Cumberland points date back to what is called the Paleolithic period, any time prior to 8,000 BCE. At the time when this point was discarded by the human who used it, Hatteras Island was not an island but a great peninsula that stretched another fourteen miles wider on the ocean side. The North Carolina sounds would have been a series of freshwater ponds

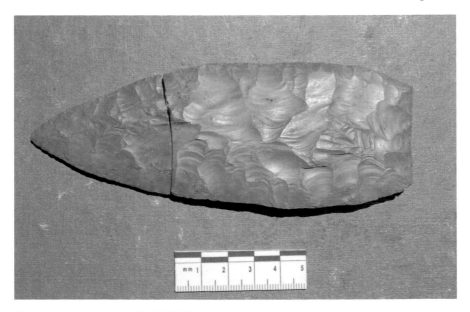

Cumberland spearhead, 11,000 BCE. *Author's collection.*

and grasslands. The rock used to make this Cumberland point is not found on Hatteras Island today. Cumberland pointed spears were used all across North America as thrusting weapons to kill large mammals. Giant walruses roamed the coast of North Carolina at the time this spearhead was created. The Earth was coming out of an ice age, and people lived in hunter-gatherer societies that used stone tools for hunting but had no agriculture. Walrus tusks have been found on Hatteras Island along with at least one bison skull and a mammoth tooth, which was donated to the Smithsonian.

Holding something so old and man-made does make the mind wonder. It is the only link we have to people from that long ago. Who was the man or woman that this spear belonged to, and what would Buxton have looked like then? Another older point was also found in Buxton by dragline operators digging a canal in 1962 but was lent to ECU to be studied and never returned. The men who found it described it to me as being shaped like a bodyboard on one end but with the nose of a surfboard, which means generally an oval with a base that arches in like a really wide letter n and a triangular point at the business end. They said it was about ten inches long. In other words, it was shaped like a Clovis point.

After the Paleolithic period comes the Archaic period, which spans from 8,000 BCE to 1,000 BCE. Hatteras Island has had archaic points turn up in Avon, Salvo, Buxton and Rodanthe. They have also been found in Nags Head and Bodie Island. Most of the archaic points that I have seen on the island are black or dark brown and not as wide as the one we found.

The fluted base of the point was to allow blood to flow out of the wound more easily than with a Cumberland point, or so it has been surmised. Very little is known about the ancient peoples of the island; we do not even know what language they spoke, but they were here. It was during the Archaic period that people began to domesticate plants and supplement the hunting and gathering with agriculture. It was also during the Archaic period that people began to build weirs to catch fish and turtles. The bow and arrow had not been invented yet, but people used another weapon called an atlatl (a spear thrower) to greatly aid in catching animals.

After the Archaic period comes what is termed the Woodland period, which can be broken up into early, middle and late. Early Woodland is considered 1,000 BCE to 200 CE, Mid-Woodland is from 201 CE to 800 CE and Late Woodland is from 800 CE to 1600. Hatteras has a fairly intact Mid-Woodland site in Frisco that dates back at least eight hundred years and another Mid-Woodland site under and behind the high school

Savannah River point, 3,000 BCE, found in Buxton. *Image by Dr. Mark Horton.*

in Buxton. In 2009 and 2011, the Frisco Mid-Woodland site had two small two-by-two-meter test pits dug by CAS/UoB. It is a shame more investigation could not have been completed because the site has since been completely ruined by construction. What little we learned is that they ate a lot of shellfish, deer, turtle and fish and that the pottery was almost exclusively sand tempered and fabric pressed, with a few cord-marked sherds turning up. No grog or bits of shell or rock was mixed in with the clay in the Mid-Woodland period. Doing so makes pottery much stronger and is one of the defining features of a Late Woodland site, along with arrowheads as opposed to only spear points.

In general, Natives from this region of North Carolina used Spanish moss or some other type of plant fibers to temper clay in the Early Woodland period. They used sand temper or tiny pebbles in the Mid-Woodland and then shell tempered in the Late Woodland. It is mainly from the pottery that we could date the Mid-Woodland site at Frisco. As expected with such an old site, it was purely a Native site with no material from other cultures. The absence of pipes at the Frisco site suggests they may not have started smoking or growing tobacco until the Late Woodland period, but the excavation was very small in scale so we don't know for sure.

Sand-tempered Mid-Woodland pottery from around 500 CE found in Frisco, North Carolina. *Author's collection.*

Many of the shells that came out of the Mid-Woodland middens in Frisco have holes drilled into them. It is likely they were used as net weights. Shellfish help demonstrate that this Mid-Woodland site was year-round. The different types of shellfish can only be found or eaten in certain seasons. For example, oysters are available from the late fall through spring, whereas clams, in particular bay clams, are only found in the summer months. Clams, oysters, scallops and whelks were all found in abundance in the midden. One midden was as large as a small hill and over 180 feet long.

After the Mid-Woodland is the Late Woodland period. This is the only period in Native American history for which we have written records to compare with the archaeology. The Late Woodland period is when the bow and arrow replaced the atlatl as the main hunting weapon. Burials changed from mounds to submerged mass graves called ossuaries. One example of a Late Woodland ossuary was the one found in 1974 in Hatteras Village by local teenagers that had at least 110 people in it.

Luckily, written records about the burial practices on Hatteras could be consulted to explain the massive pile of bones. The Indians on Hatteras/

Croatoan in the 1580s had two types of burial practices, one of which is described in detail by Thomas Harriot in his 1590 publication *A Brief and True Report of the New Found Land of Virginia*. In summary, the bodies of those who died in a given year were put on scaffolding inside a morgue called a machucomick and left to decompose until a special date, when the bones were publicly removed and polished with bear grease and then placed all together in a mass grave. A ceremony took place, and an idol called Kewas sat in the morgue. The machucomicks looked like scaffolding with a raised platform nine or ten feet high, on which the row of dead bodies were laid. Next to the corpses was Kewas (pronounced *kee-vas*). The Kewas idol was made of clay and wood; was painted black, white and red; and wore a copper and shell necklace. These idols were about three feet high and had a human form in a sitting or squatting position. They were used by several tribes in the southeastern portion of the United States.

Knowing that the disarticulation of the bones was on purpose and part of the burial process helps the archaeologists make sense of the find. In the 1974 discovery, the bones did have some order to them. The skulls were in rows and the long bones in bundles, according to the local residents who first stumbled onto the burial ground.

Chapter 10

THE REAL SEARCH BEGINS

November 2009

After much e-mail correspondence, in November 2009, Professor Horton and PhD candidate Louisa Pittman came to Hatteras Island and conducted eight test pits in varying areas on the island, including Buxton and Frisco. However, only three test pits gave us any archaeology of interest: two at the Jennette's Creek area of Buxton and one in Frisco. In Buxton, one test pit was mostly Croatoan with some European context mixed in, and the other was mostly colonial with a bit of Native material. Frisco was a purely Native site that turned out to be Mid-Woodland. The Frisco site had come and gone long before the arrival of Europeans. I was simply taking the archaeologists where I had two things: permission to dig and where I had seen pottery uncovered before either from construction or erosion. It takes a trained professional to know the difference between pot sherds that are over one thousand years old versus three hundred years old. While the Frisco site was ancient, the Buxton site was right on the money for the contact period based on the pottery. A perfect sequence of colonial artifacts from 1750 down to 1650 was found mixed with Native material, meaning the sixteenth century was just below these finds waiting to be dug up.

Just as when John White was about to reach the colony, we, too, were interrupted by a storm. Hurricane Ida hit Hatteras Island on Friday, November 13, 2009. The rain bands began before dawn. We had a tarp in the test pit and a homemade pump run off a car battery to suck out water.

The winds picked up and pushed the sound into the creeks and across the island, and some parts flooded. The water level rose and began to flood our trench so that any deeper was hitting mud.

It was exciting to be out in that wind and rain trying to finish the excavation, but I thought my heart was going to stop when out of the wet bottom of the trench came a human mandible (jawbone) that still had some teeth in it and then skull fragments and other various human bones. I could tell the experts were on high stress, so along with the rest of the volunteers, I left them in the trench and went to sort shells and wash artifacts found earlier, including some really cool French gunflints. The bones were disarticulated, basically in a big pile. Clearly, this was another disarticulated burial like the one discovered in Hatteras Village in 1974, only this was different. This grave had to contain the remains of people more recently deceased than the ones from Hatteras Village, which dated to 1395, because a perfect sequence of artifacts in context led down to about 1650 just before the human bones were discovered. Also impossible to ignore was that a handful of European artifacts—including an unfired musket ball, a piece of earthenware and a pipe that was of an ambiguous origin—appeared to have been tossed into the grave.

If these remains were of Croatoan Indians who died sometime prior to 1640 and they had been around seventy when they died, they would have been young adults when the English voyages in the 1580s took place. It is likely that these Indians at the very least knew Manteo, given how small the tribe was. Had we passed through the missing century of the 1600s back into recorded history? The human bones were sent to the state archaeologist department in Raleigh, as required by law. The UoB team had seen enough to commit to a full-scale dig the following spring in conjunction with the CAS.

We found out months later from the State of North Carolina that the bones belonged to three individuals: two adults and a child. No DNA testing was done, but the North Carolina Office of State Archaeology (OSA) determined the bones to be of Native origin by physical examination.

Also mixed in the mud were lots of deer bones and some coyote teeth. The bones were in a sealed layer beneath the shell midden we had been excavating for two days. It seemed odd for a burial to later have a midden on top of it, which could indicate the burial was much older than the midden. The midden itself helped preserve the bones below. Hatteras has a lot of silica in the sandy soil, which is not good for preserving bones, but the calcium from the thick layer of shells in the midden above the bones probably helped

Earthenware, sixteenth century. *Author's collection.*

counteract the rapid decay that would have occurred otherwise. Answers to a lot of questions would have to wait.

Hurricane Ida washed out the only road on or off the island in Rodanthe, about thirty miles north of us, trapping the English archaeologists, who were scheduled to leave the next day. Leave they did, but on an hour-long ferry ride to Ocracoke and then another two-and-a-half-hour ferry ride to the mainland, from where they drove an extra one hundred miles to get to their flight. Yet they still left happy and eager to return.

As exciting as the finds were in 2009, the bones were never dated by the state or tested to see if they could have perhaps been half English, given the fact that they were buried with English items sometime prior to 1650. It is very possible that the English items found with the bones were simply traded to the tribe sometime in the early 1600s. Much was left to speculation in 2009.

At least one of the adults found was male. His femur bone measured longer than one of the UoB students who stands at six feet, four inches tall. The child was determined by the discovery of baby teeth. All of the artifacts, minus the human remains, were put on display in Buxton where they were found.

Chapter 11

DAUB GONE IT

2010

In an effort to avoid the grave site out of respect, the 2010 dig moved away from the human remains site of 2009, focusing instead on the European homestead that was also located in 2009. Instead of two-by-two-meter test pits, five-by-three-meter trenches were dug with the aid of CAS volunteers and graduate students from UoB. Professor Mark Horton and grad student Louisa Pittman (who had conducted the 2009 dig) led the charge again. Within the first hour, huge clumps of daub, bricks and European ceramics were uncovered.

This homestead had coins, glass bottles and English ceramics that made it very easy to date. The French and Indian War–age home was timber framed, and the walls were made of daub. Daub is a sand-clay mixture much like a type of plaster. Huge clumps of daub were found in massive quantities, enough to fill fourteen five-gallon buckets. One piece of daub had a piece of salt glaze English plate still stuck in the side of it, making the date range of the house very easy. The dark square in the middle of the picture was a well that still had some of the barrel in it. It was so fragile that we left the barrel intact when we backfilled the trenches.

Salt glaze pottery began being manufactured in England in the seventeenth century and by 1720 in Yorktown, Virginia, meaning the construction of the house is within the date range of the pottery found in the wall. Coins also helped to narrow down a date for the homestead.

We found a silver piece of eight from a Spanish pillar dollar. They were minted in Mexico and date from the 1730s to the 1770s. The money

The barrel found in a 1740 homestead. *Author's collection.*

supply was so low in the colonies that coins were cut into eight equal pieces and then used as currency. An English ha'penny was also found with the date 1737 on it and a profile of King George II. Together with slipware (1675–1770) and jackfield-ware (1740–90), as well as some delft (1630–1790), the coins and other artifacts make it safe to say this was an early to mid-eighteenth-century home. The house probably stood for at least a generation. One of the strangest finds to come out of the house was the head and jawbones of a horse that were found under the floor. It was customary for some subcultures in England to bury a horse head under the room in which people danced.

Pigs' teeth, bore tusks and horse and cattle bones, along with bones of chicken and other animals from the Old World, were abundant. The amount of Native American material at this layer was very little, reinforcing the land-grabbing theory going on in the mid-1700s.

One very interesting Croatoan find was a whelk shell hoe used for farming. The beak of the whelk has been grinded down to a nub from use as a hoe to till the land. The drilled hole where a wooden handle once went in has a notch in it to help the shell snap into the wooden pole in addition to being tied to the pole. We now have more of these, but the one pictured was the

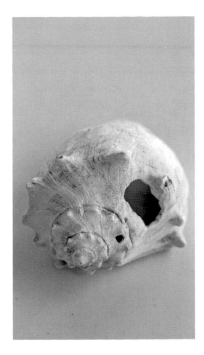

Above, left: Salt glaze pottery found embedded in daub. *Photo by Caroline Jarvis.*

Above, right: A whelk shell hoe called a rashaquan by the Croatoan. *Author's collection.*

Middle: A silver piece of eight minted in Mexico from a Spanish pillar dollar. *Photo by Caroline Jarvis.*

Bottom: A 1737 English ha'penny. *Author's collection.*

first to be found. The Croatoan and other coastal tribes also used shell tools to build canoes. They had no iron and thus had to burn trees to the ground rather than cut them down. The trees were then burned for a time and the layer of ash scraped out with shells like this whelk. This process of burning and scraping was repeated until the tree became a canoe. It was very labor intensive, and therefore, it is no surprise that of all the things the Europeans had when they made initial contact with Native peoples, saws, axes and hatches were among the most desired by the Natives. Thomas Harriot tells us that in 1585, the Natives were growing corn, squash, beans, cucumbers, sunflowers, tobacco, peas and pumpkins.

Around the 1740ish homestead and under it, we started to find more Croatoan artifacts and a little bit older English artifacts like delft, stoneware and kaolin tobacco pipes. English pipes at the time were made from kaolin, a type of white clay found in England but not North Carolina. They were also wire bored, unlike the Croatoan pipes, which were bored with reeds or sticks. Sometimes the Native pipes had clay bowls but reed stems. We found a Croatoan pipe that still has tobacco residue inside it!

The animal bones we were finding changed from pigs and chickens to a more Native diet of local animals such as deer, shellfish and lots of turtle and fish.

Another interesting find was that of a bow-drill stone, the first of many we would find in years to come. Bow drills were used to start fires. A stick was placed onto a dry piece of wood, and then the string of a bow was looped around the stick. The bow was moved back and forth, causing the

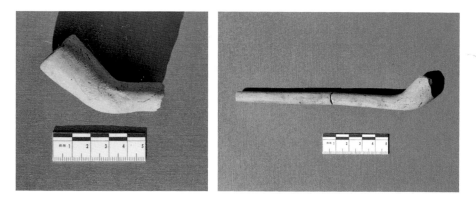

Left: A Croatoan ceremonial pipe. *Photo by Dr. Mark Horton.*

Right: A kaolin English pipe that has been wire bored. *Photo by Dr. Mark Horton.*

Bow drill stones. *Photo by Caroline Jarvis.*

stick to spin while a stone was placed on top to keep the stick from falling over and to provide pressure. The result was that the stick spun in place on the dry piece of wood, creating enough friction to start a fire. Spanish moss and other easily lit materials went around the base of the stick.

We had reached the missing century again. The site was full of hundreds of Croatoan pottery sherds and piles of shellfish. The English pipes, ceramics and occasional iron object were minimal but constant. This meant that during the missing century, the Croatoan were thriving and had contact with Europeans directly or trade from Jamestown (founded in 1607 in Virginia) was trickling down to the island or both. It was also possible that a few Europeans were living with the tribe. Many shipwrecks have occurred on Hatteras Island. In fact, when the English arrived at Hatteras in 1584, they were shown a shipwreck (probably Spanish or French) by the Natives that had wrecked twenty-six years prior. The English had two shipwrecks off Hatteras in the 1580s (the *Tiger* and the *Francis*). The idea of a few castaways, pirates or runaway indentured servants living on

Left: Horse bridle. *Author's collection.*

Below: Part of an English naval officer's shoe buckle. *Author's collection.*

Hatteras in the 1600s with the Croatoan Indians is certainly possible, but the handful of English items we were getting did not prove or disprove this idea. What we had found was English stuff from the 1600s in what was clearly a Native village; how it got there was not answered until later. We were all excited to see what came next as we pushed into the 1500s.

Then it happened again; more disarticulated human remains were unearthed, and again they had English artifacts tossed in just above the bones. This time there was a horse bridle, shoe buckle with part of the word "Chatham" etched in it and an unfired musket ball. The 2010 dig was a lot dryer with no hurricane, and the bones were once again sent to Raleigh. It appears to have been another clearly disarticulated pile of bones, much like what was discovered in 2009. It ate up the rest of the time our archaeologists had before they had to leave, and we again went no deeper.

The buckle or piece of buckle we found was not for a belt but rather a shoe. As luck would have it, the piece we found had the word "Chatham" etched into it. Chatham was a naval yard in England on the Thames River, and this type of shoe buckle was used by naval officers.

At least in 2010, there was no hurricane to delay the English departure from the island. Instead, a volcano erupted in Iceland that delayed all flights to England for a week due to the enormous amounts of ash. Once again, the UoB crew was stranded for a little extra time. We had already backfilled our trenches, so instead of digging, the extra time was spent cleaning artifacts and gooping together Croatoan pottery. "Gooping" is a made-up term for gluing pottery sherds that fit together. The actual adhesive used to put pottery back together is called goop and is mainly used in plumbing but serves perfectly for our purpose because it is clear.

African colonial ware found in Croatoan village. *Author's collection.*

Animal bones—fish, deer, birds and turtles. *Author's collection.*

We found a sand-tempered bowl in a Late Woodland context and pieced it back together. It contains four mending holes, or small holes drilled near the rim of the vessel on either side of a crack. The two holes were then bound together by plant fiber cordage to help seal the crack. This bowl was one of the very few examples of Native pottery on Hatteras that was neither shell-tempered nor decorated. It is similar to colonial ware made by African slaves in Jamestown. Were the Croatoan harboring a runaway slave? It appears they might have been.

Our first full-scale dig was a success and started to shed some light on the lost century of the 1600s. We now knew that the Indians here were well fed and had some access to English goods. We never reached beyond the 1650s in 2010 because once again human remains appeared and the rest of the time we had was spent carefully excavating them. The English items buried with them were actually about an inch above the bones and remain a puzzling mystery. We were really in for a shock the following year in 2011.

Only one arrowhead was found, and it appears the Natives may have converted completely to guns based on all the flint and lead shot found in the middens and the lack of arrowheads. It was noted by English explorers in the 1580s that sometimes stingray barbs were used instead of napped rock arrowheads. We did find a few stingray barbs, but because the animal was also eaten, it is impossible to tell if the barbs were used as arrowheads. The barbs did not require construction to create and were/are abundant on Hatteras Island. What we do know is that lead shot from guns was being used by the tribe in the 1600s. The number of animal bones we found demonstrates the Croatoan were thriving.

Chapter 12

MYSTERIOUS WOMAN

2011

In 2011, we decided to finish up the 1740s-age homestead and did so, finding much more of the same sort of English ceramics from the 2010 dig. One special find was a beautiful metallic glaze jar. We also found a lot of orange and yellow slipware, possibly produced in England but most likely from Philadelphia. Both were found in a mid-eighteenth-century context.

At least there were no hurricanes or volcanoes to worry about in 2011. However, our English friends decided to fly in and out of Raleigh instead of Norfolk, Virginia, that year, and tornadoes did strike the Raleigh area, killing over thirty people.

Each morning when we arrived to dig, the site was littered with deer tracks and deer droppings. The weather was beautiful, and all you could hear were the sounds of leaves rustling in the wind and birds singing. The Spanish moss hanging from the live oaks and wildflowers made me wonder if the backdrop had looked and sounded the same four hundred years ago in the Croatoan village.

After digging a little deeper, we came to the most shocking find yet. Under the sand came a flex burial of a Croatoan girl about twenty years old. This was the closest any of us will ever come to seeing a Croatoan Indian. Her wrists and ankles were tied with leather, and she had a hematite hatchet buried with her. It still is. The state by this point knew it was clearly a Native burial and had the common sense to let us say a few words and respectfully rebury this woman, unmoved and unmolested by our hands.

Left: Metallic jug, eighteenth century. *Author's collection.*

Below: Slipware, eighteenth century. *Author's collection.*

Other burials of this sort have been found within sixty miles of Hatteras Island in Currituck and Wanchese, as well as other parts of North Carolina. What determined if a person got this type of burial versus the mass grave (called an ossuary) is still not known. What we do know is that age and gender did not play a role in the burial practices because all ages and both genders have been found in both burial types on Hatteras Island and in other parts of North Carolina.

This woman was lying on her right side facing west. One cannot help but wonder who she was. How did she die? We will probably never know. She stood about five feet, eight inches and had just gotten her wisdom teeth. Her name, life and death remain a mystery. I said a prayer in Algonquian to her, and she was respectfully reburied. *Winkan nupes*! (Sleep well.)

Based on the English artifacts found in a midden that sealed the burial, this woman probably died around 1630. She was probably part of the generation after initial contact with Europeans. If she was twenty when she died in the 1630s, then she was born around 1610, just twenty-three years after the colony arrived. She may have even been the offspring of a colonist and a Croatoan.

This woman may have known Manteo or been related to him. We do not know how old Manteo was when the English met him in 1584, but he was probably in his mid-twenties or thirties. The only description given of him is that he was a lusty fellow, meaning healthy. Manteo could have been as young as forty when this girl was born or as old as seventy, but it is almost certain that he knew her, given how small the tribe on the island was. We will never know, but as I looked at her lying there in the sand, I could not help but ponder the possibilities.

The burial was different from the disarticulate bones we found the previous two years, not only because we could see a true human form but also because this woman would be left unmolested where we found her, and there was a comforting peace in that. I have heard too many stories of graves being discovered by bulldozers building houses and pushed aside or placed in trash bags and moved by construction workers. The Croatoan tribe, like a majority of tribes, is not federally recognized and therefore powerless today. If bones of unrecognized tribes are found in North Carolina, they almost always go unreported.

Once again, skeletal remains ate up most of the time the archaeologists had, and we went no deeper. The University of Bristol students who did a vast majority of the laborious digging were limited to their spring break. We did not know it at the time, but later, as more flex burials were found, they were always covered with a shell midden. A lot of people on the island today will cover a grave site with whelk shells, which may be a tradition passed on by the Croatoan or simply a coincidence. There is nothing written in the primary sources about marking graves with shells, so it is also possible this tradition began sometime just after the sixteenth century.

Chapter 13

GUNS AND BRANDY

In 2012, we were determined not to find skeletons and finally reach the 1500s, so we moved at least a mile to another Late Woodland site in Buxton. Immediately, we started to find Croatoan pipes and pottery alongside tiny lead shot balls and loads of English gunflints and a few random iron objects. As we dug a little deeper, there came decorative pipe bowls that were made in America by the famous pipe manufacturer Emmanuel Drew between 1650 and 1669. After sifting the sand a second time through fine mesh and water, we also found glass trade beads from about 1660. We created a rectangular wooden frame and lined the bottom with mosquito mesh. We then lowered the sand into the water and gently moved back and forth. Oddly, this method seemed to attract sea turtles, which constantly tried to mount the sifter.

We also found the postholes of the longhouses and possibly a smokehouse. There were a few very odd things found, like a Dutch coin weight from 1648 that was used to weigh against a Scottish gold penny from 1644. Other rare finds were a copper key to a pocket watch, a gun barrel and some very old glass that, as we discovered later, predated 1600.

In a small two-by-two-meter test pit, we found the bones from hundreds of animals. We were putting a small hole in a massive pile of animal bones, the extent of which is unknown, as we did not extend the trench. Over sixty adult turtles were found just in this small pit. It must have been quite a feast. The date of this feast appears to have been just after the nearby inlet closed

Top: Wet sieving. *Author's collection.*

Middle: Coin weights produced in Holland. The square one on the left was used to weigh against a gold Scottish penny from 1644. *Author's collection.*

Bottom: All of these bones are from one two-by-two-meter pit. *Author's collection.*

Lead shot and lead shot waste. *Author's collection.*

in 1713. It is speculated the feast could have been a celebration of the end of the Tuscarora War, which ended in 1714. The Hatteras tribe aided the North Carolina colony and helped fight the Tuscarora. They were granted sixteen bushels of corn from the colonial stock as a thank-you. Perhaps this feast was a celebration, or they may have simply hunted more animals when the inlet closed, as that would have reduced the number of shellfish in the area. Inlets are always a breeding ground for shellfish. We will never know the reason for the feast, but judging by the number of brandy bottles and animal bones, Dr. Horton joked it may have been the biggest party ever thrown on Hatteras Island.

The Croatoan were making their own lead shot from stone molds by at least 1650, if not earlier. This means they must have had guns, which would make them the first tribe to use guns and cast their own shot. The lead shot we found in 2012 was less than one hundred feet from a 1580s gunlock, the oldest English gun found in America.

Also found were more onion jars, which probably contained brandy. In fact, besides lead shot, the most common European artifacts found in the Croatoan village sites are liquor bottles, usually brandy. The two-by-two-meter pit we dug on this huge pile of bones and liquor was nicknamed the party pit. After digging a little deeper in the party pit, a few older and

A brandy bottle. *Author's collection.*

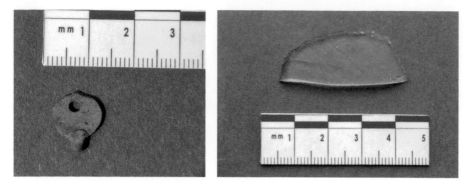

Left: A pocket watch key. *Photo by Mark Horton.*

Right: Lead light glass, sixteenth century. *Author's collection.*

surprising artifacts emerged. The most significant find from the party pit was a piece of glass from the sixteenth century. After analysis from an XRF machine, it was determined that this glass contained high levels of potassium and was not cheaply made. The edge had been snipped. It was a piece of lead light glass.

Near the glass was some stoneware that was made in both the sixteenth and seventeenth centuries. It appeared we had finally reached the sixteenth century. Croatoan pottery and pipes were mixed in the same layer as the stoneware and lead light glass.

The story of the missing century (1600s) appears to be that the Croatoan were thriving and very well fed based on the middens. They were using iron tools and English guns, wearing pocket watches and drinking brandy. In other words, we had evidence of assimilation going on at least as early as 1650 and possibly earlier.

While the party pit was being excavated, a larger trench was being dug thirty feet away where auger holes had shown evidence of another midden. Attention turned to this trench when postholes of a possible smokehouse were discovered. A smokehouse was a holy place for the Croatoan. The entrance of a smokehouse always faced east toward the rising sun, where life begins. Hell, called Popogusso, was believed to be here on Earth where the sun sets.

The smokehouse building itself was like a very small wooden igloo that one had to crawl to enter. In the dirt floor of the smokehouse was a fire pit. The person who entered was to throw tobacco onto the fire and send a question or wish to be carried up to God by the smoke of the

Stoneware, sixteenth or seventeenth century. *Author's collection.*

revered plant. When new weir nets were built, they were blessed with tobacco that was thrown into the water and the air. When the fire pit of the apparent smokehouse was excavated, it smelled richly of tobacco. The tobacco smoked in the United States today was brought over from the West Indies by John Rolfe in 1609; the tobacco that was indigenous to North Carolina contained as much as nine times the nicotine of regular tobacco and was a mild hallucinogenic. The plant itself was revered by the Croatoan, but by 1650, there is some evidence of a change in tobacco culture. Archaeologist Fred Nevall Jones, part of the UoB team, had insight on the change in Native pipes from post-1650 versus pre-1650. The pipes prior to about 1650 had very large bowls, indicating communal use, where the pipe was passed around among a group of people. By contrast, the pipes found post-1650 had smaller bowls and stems and were probably used by individuals for personal use. The change in the type of tobacco being smoked as well as European influence could account for this change in tobacco culture, but this theory needs more investigation. Having nine times as much nicotine actually makes the tobacco less addictive. The body craves a certain level of nicotine once it is introduced, and one must smoke nine times as much of the West Indies tobacco to reach that level.

Top: Starfish pipe bowl. *Author's collection.*

Bottom: Tidewater pipe bowl. *Author's collection.*

The less harsh strain of tobacco brought into Virginia from the West Indies in the early 1600s also ushered in wire-bored pipe stems and pipe bowls made from molds. The Emmanuel Drew and other wire-bored pipes found in the Croatoan village site show remarkable artwork that mimics some of the common patterns found on Native pottery.

Decorated Tidewater pipe bowls were made in Virginia and Maryland from 1611 to 1650. A common pipe we found had a starfish pattern on the bowl of the pipe. The starfish-patterned ones were also found on Hatteras by archaeologist William Haag in the 1950s but were misidentified as being Native.

The Croatoan village really started to take shape once we began to find postholes of the buildings and could mark out where buildings once

Postholes of a Croatoan longhouse. *Author's collection.*

stood. As we continued to dig, we found lots of buildings. We would get more than our fill of postholes on future digs, with a final count over six hundred. At this point we were just on the edge of what was the center of town for Croatoan.

Inside the longhouses we always found fire pits that were usually a large oval shape and were common in longhouses found near Jamestown as well.

What is under this missing century layer? We had a good find with the lead light glass and were eager to continue at that depth. We stopped digging just shy of finding out because a tiny glass bead was found. Everyone was disappointed at this discovery. It meant we had probably missed some tiny artifacts that had passed through our sifters. To correct this mistake, we had to resift all the dirt through mosquito mesh and water. As much as everyone wanted to continue deeper, it would have to wait. The result of resifting was a lot more glass trade beads from the mid-1600s, along with thousands of small lead shot, a few more pieces of copper of an uncertain origin and a few more decorated pipe bowl fragments. These let us know we were still in the mid-1600s. The wet sifting was a long, tedious process that could not have been completed without the aid of CAS members and other local volunteers.

We know from the written record that glass trade beads were exchanged for pearls in the 1580s. Later in Charleston, South Carolina, 240 pounds

Glass beads from Italy, 1650. *Photo by Dr. Mark Horton.*

of these beads were brought over from England to be traded in 1670. The beads we found are at least a decade older than that and littered the Croatoan village site. In Virginia, John Smith was able to trade a pound or two of blue beads for two hundred bushels of corn in 1607. The blue beads were of the highest value to the Natives because of a type of shell jewelry monetary system that already existed in the New World. In this shell monetary system, blue shell beads were valued the most and came from being drilled out of the foot of quahog clam shells. The tubular part of whelk shells was used to make tubular-shaped white beads.

These glass beads would not have been worn as a necklace but rather were sewn into fabric that decayed long ago, leaving only the glass behind. Look at how small some of them are. No one can say the CAS and UoB were not thorough, as we found hundreds of these. It turns out our beads were made in Venice and came to Hatteras via the English. We also found one with Josh Gates during the filming of an episode of *Expedition Unknown* for the Travel Channel. Also found were more copper items, which the Croatoan valued most of all.

When the English first contacted the Croatoan in 1584, the Native people with political authority and influence wore copper ornaments. It was immediately recognized by the English that copper would yield a great trade in the New World. In fact, one copper pot could be traded for as many as fifty deerskins. In turn, just ten of those skins could be sold in England for as

Above, left: The size and shape of this gunflint was for a pistol. The gray color suggests it is English. Honey-colored French ones were also found. *Author's collection.*

Above, right: Snipped copper. *Author's collection.*

Left: Croatoan copper earrings. *Author's collection.*

much as a sailor would make in a year. Due to the profits the English could make from copper, they brought a lot of copper with them to trade, which makes it very hard to tell the origin of copper artifacts, since the Natives also had copper before the English arrived.

All of the copper we found on this dig was simple rectangles, ear cuffs, earrings or small tubes made from rolling a flat piece of copper. One of the copper bars we found looks as if it were snipped. This is indicative of the use of an iron tool. We also found a fireplace hook made of iron. This type of item was not the sort of thing typically brought over for trade but rather for use. Its presence in a Croatoan midden is a little mysterious. Mixed in with the metals were gunflints.

Even the copper the Croatoan tribe got locally had to come from tribes over one hundred miles away because there is no source of copper on the Outer Banks. The same thing is true of the clay used to make pottery and even the rocks used to make arrowheads. The Croatoan and other tidewater-area tribes had extensive trade networks that reached all the way to the mountains. Conversely, the coast had many shell products and medicinal plants that the Natives in the mountains wanted.

The Croatoan and many Native Americans are unfairly stereotyped as eking out a living from the land and living a barbaric, primitive life. In reality, the Croatoan had agriculture; lived in houses and towns; had organized government and religion; traded extensively with other tribes; and lived long, healthy lives. They knew the Earth was round and that it went around the sun long before Europeans did. Thomas Harriot, the English scientist/mathematician who lived with the Natives for a year in 1585, even suggested that the Native diet be copied by the English because they were so "long lived."

By the end of our two-week dig in 2012, we had reasons to believe we might find a slightly older layer just a few meters away and knew before we left exactly where to go next. Finally, the next year we hit the sixteenth century we had all been waiting for, and what we found exceeded the hopes of even the most optimistic among us.

Chapter 14

PAY DIRT

W e started by extending the last pit we dug in 2012 that had such beautifully preserved postholes from a Croatoan longhouse or some other Native structure. The postholes were sealed beneath a lovely midden layer that had the usual bone, shell and Native pottery in it, along with a few lead shot balls and some buckleyware, which meant the midden above the postholes dated to the early seventeenth century. We did not expect to find any European culture under the midden but hoped to map out the shape of a few longhouses.

We were wrong on both accounts. The longhouse we hoped to find ended up being 417 postholes from which no one could make any definite conclusions about the shape of the structures. The theory at the moment is that the postholes represent several structures that blew down and were then put back up in roughly the same spot, thus creating a real mess for archaeologists. Hatteras Island is a very windy, storm-riddled place, so the idea that homes had to be repaired or rebuilt from time to time is a reasonable assertion. Occasionally, we did find a clean oval pattern.

Also at this layer was a great deal more copper than we had found anywhere else on the island and some stoneware that dates to the sixteenth century. The stoneware at such a purely Native layer made everyone begin to question if we had finally reached the sixteenth century. Then came another remarkable discovery. Part of a copper bun that showed clear evidence of smelting copper came out of the ground next to an iron firebar. The Croatoan did not smelt copper and did not have any iron. The stoneware was beginning not to look like a red herring after all. Then another chunk of smelted coper was found that fit perfectly into the first one.

According to the National Park Service, the greatest finds ever made on Roanoke Island were of a science center that is believed to be from 1585. Joachim Ganz, a German metallurgist, accompanied the English in 1585 to test New World metals. A site on Roanoke Island had produced chunks of copper slag, suggesting someone worked with copper ore there. They also found three Nuremberg tokens along with crucibles used to melt the ores. The tokens more than anything else were the best evidence of any sixteenth-century English presence on Roanoke Island. Unfortunately, they were not found in context because they were disturbed in the 1950s when the earthworks of what the NPS has named Fort Raleigh were built on Roanoke Island. One of the other chief finds on Roanoke Island was a copper aiglet (tip of a fancy shoelace).

So naturally, after finding German stoneware and smelted copper on Hatteras Island, Dr. Horton and Nick Knowles of the BBC decided it would be a good idea to get a look at what had been found on Roanoke Island to compare. A quick tour was arranged with the National Park Service of the Roanoke finds, and then the dig on Hatteras continued. The prize finds held on Roanoke were three Nuremberg tokens, along with copper slag and crucibles.

The very next day (Good Friday), March 29, Nick Knowles pulled a Nuremberg token *identical* to one of the ones found on Roanoke Island out of a sifter that was only a few feet away from where the smelted copper bun had been found and in the same layer. This was the first stratified Hans Shultes Nuremberg token ever found in the New World. The first token ever found also came from Hatteras Island back in 1938 and was given to archaeologist J.C. Harrington, who found three more tokens on Roanoke in the 1950s, two of which matched the one originally found on Hatteras. The token CAS and UoB found in 2013 matched the other token. I know this is confusing, so let me put it another way. A dime is found on Hatteras, then two dimes and a penny are found on Roanoke and then a penny is found on Hatteras. There are thousands of different types of tokens, each with different makers and designs. What we have now are exactly two and only two of those types found on Roanoke and the same two types now found on Hatteras. None of these types of tokens has been found in Jamestown or anywhere else in America. The chance that these tokens are not from the same source is astronomical. Also, all five tokens have holes punched in them so they can be strung and would make a great trade item to the Indians who valued copper the way Europeans valued gold. The tokens are actually a copper and zinc alloy. The Nuremberg token connection between Fort Raleigh and Hatteras has been established for over fifty years, but none of the tokens were found stratified, and until that happened, there would always be some doubt about when they arrived. Now one has been found stratified, and in a Croatoan village no less, also near copper smelting! These discoveries strengthen if not solidify the idea that the English in the sixteenth century were working copper on both Hatteras and Roanoke Islands.

Along with the tokens, one of the better finds on Roanoke was a copper aiglet. We found one on Hatteras identical to the one on Roanoke in the same layer as the token, smelted copper bun, German stoneware and iron ingot. Later, we found several more aiglets. At this point, everyone got excited, and the artifacts continued to pour out of the pit, including two brass scabbard tips from daggers, a silver-plated ring and two of the best arrowheads ever found on the island. Little did we know during our excitement that the best finds were still a year away. This year's dig was not through with us yet though. It was as if the earth heard what the National Park Service said on Roanoke and gave us matching finds in one morning that surpassed everything found on Roanoke in over one hundred digs. The fact that everything found on Roanoke matches finds on Hatteras is indicative of them coming from the same source.

Copper aiglet. *Author's collection.*

Left: Smelted copper bun, sixteenth century. *Author's collection.*

Right: Germanic stoneware jug, sixteenth century. *Author's collection.*

The copper aiglets used on the tips of English shoelaces in the sixteenth century may have been repurposed and worn as copper beads by the Croatoan. The one found on Roanoke matched the dozen found on Hatteras Island. Dr. Horton believes they were repurposed as decorative beads because so many were found in one tiny spot that they might have been a necklace or simply collected by the Natives. The copper bun looked like it had been beaten and was almost two inches thick in the middle.

The particular piece of German stoneware we found from the late 1500s was part of the rim of a jug and the most easily datable part of the ceramic. It once had a silver ring that capped the top of it. This was an expensive jug at the time.

It is amazing how different iron artifacts look after undergoing electrolysis. Once the rust is removed, the iron artifacts are dipped in acetone, dried and coated in a special wax to keep air out. After finding the brass apostles, Dr. Horton did some research and found that one had also been discovered in California at a place called Drake's Cove. The cove is named after Sir Francis Drake, who spent some time there in the 1580s as part of his trip around the world. Drake's last stop on the trip before returning to England was…Hatteras Island.

The importance of what we were finding was only matched by what we were not finding. The decorative pipe bowls and glass beads we had been finding constantly had vanished. We had finally reached the late 1500s, yet European artifacts continued to be found. As explained earlier, the English had spent time on Croatoan/Hatteras in 1584 as well

Top: Firebar before electrolysis, sixteenth century. *Author's collection.*

Middle: Firebar after electrolysis, sixteenth century. *Author's collection.*

Bottom: Brass apostle that held gunpowder, sixteenth century. *Author's collection.*

Top: Nuremberg token, sixteenth century, found in Buxton. *Author's collection.*

Bottom: English gun barrel. It was possibly repurposed as a chisel to hollow out trees to build canoes. One end has been hammered in, and the other end has been cut at an angle to make it sharp. The inside of the barrel was full of pine pitch. *Author's collection.*

as 1585 and 1587. In order to prove these artifacts came from the 1587 colony as opposed to men from 1585 or 1584, we needed more, but this was a beautiful start.

The copper bun was found in the middle of a longhouse. Lead shot and bits of glass and iron accompanied the main finds at this level. We were digging a trench the size of two parking spaces, so it is amazing so much was yielded.

We finally found a gun to go with all the lead shot—well, a gun barrel at least. It had been beaten and cut on one end at a forty-five-degree angle. Perhaps it was repurposed as a metal tool once it broke.

We now had sixteenth-century artifacts at a sixteenth-century layer, meaning they got there in the sixteenth century. Sixteenth-century English artifacts had been found before on Hatteras Island but in a seventeenth-century context. We still had one problem though: how do you tell the difference between artifacts from 1587 (the year of the Lost Colony) and artifacts from 1585 or 1584? Both the 1584 and 1585 English voyages spent time on Hatteras Island.

We needed something the 1584 and 1585 voyages would not have left behind, such as a gentleman's sword or saker cannon. Neither cannon nor this type of sword would have been traded or left behind by the groups in 1584 or 1585. In fact, Captain Barlowe of the 1584 voyage wrote down that they would not part with any of their swords. The other find that would separate 1587 from the other sixteenth-century voyages would be something from a female colonist. The 1587 Lost Colony was the only English voyage in that century that brought women to the New World.

Chapter 15

THE EARTH LISTENS

We decided we needed to figure out exactly the boundaries of the Croatoan village we were on. Trying to figure out the size and shape of the Indian village would be impossible if you attempted to dig trench after trench until you reached sterile soil. After doing a series of auger holes (posthole-size holes), we discovered the Indian village seemed to basically run parallel to a creek that no longer exists for about a mile, with very little material found on the other side of the now dry creek, which became low and marshy. The village also extended smack into the Pamlico Sound, so there is really no telling how far it extended in that direction because so much of that land has been lost to erosion. What we are digging on is essentially the southern end, a mere ribbon of the village that sat between the sound and a creek in a relatively high wooded area— high being only twenty-three feet above sea level today and in some places as low as fourteen feet.

We located a large midden by the auger hole method. Much like the game Battleship, when you get a hit you focus on that area and open up a trench. More of the same mountains of shellfish, turtle bones, deer bones and Native pottery came out of our latest trench. There was also an enormous amount of lead shot and no arrowheads. We got to the glass bead level, which contained more of the decorated pipes, bits of copper and iron. The artifacts were 90 percent Croatoan, as expected, considering it was their village. From the European artifacts coming out, it was clear this midden dated to about 1650. There were a few new things found, such as the lead net weights and knife handles made out of deer antlers with cool crisscross patterns carved on them.

We found quite a few large square nails covered in rust and other unidentified iron objects due to the balls of rust around them. One iron item in particular looked interesting. Some of the students thought it was a fancy door hinge or some sort of decorative piece of iron. Dr. Horton held it with a smile and asked me what I thought it was, and half joking, I said a rapier sword handle. Dr. Horton nodded yes and said that is exactly what it was.

I had that feeling you get when you miss a stair in the dark and your heart jumps. If this was true, it would be huge. In the 1990s, a couple of sixteenth-century English artifacts had turned up in a Croatoan village, but it was not clear if they had arrived in 1584 or 1585 or from the infamous 1587 Lost Colony. Identifying and dating an artifact is one thing, but trying to decipher between three years is almost impossible. The stuff found in the 1990s was also found in a seventeenth-century stratus or layer in the ground surrounded by seventeenth-century artifacts. All this means is that the older stuff was hung onto for a few decades before it was discarded, or older stuff was brought in at a later date. The problem we had been having with our finds was that while we had found sixteenth-century English artifacts in a pure sixteenth-century layer (meaning they for sure got there in the sixteenth century), that still did not tell us the difference between 1584 and 1587; all we knew was 15-something. Short of the body of a colonist, there was only one thing we could find that would tell us it came in 1587 as opposed to 1584, and that was a sword.

Arthur Barlowe, the captain of the 1584 voyage that spent six weeks on Hatteras Island, recorded in a letter to the queen's court historian, Richard Hakluyt, that while the Natives would have traded anything for a sword, they would not part with any so as to keep the true value a secret. Some would argue that all this stuff was traded from Jamestown and that those colonists brought over old guns and swords and then traded them to Virginia Indians, who then traded to other Indians until they made their way down to Hatteras. Yet no swords or guns of this age have been found in Jamestown or anywhere between Jamestown and Hatteras, so this theory is pretty baseless. The only place weapons of this age have been found is Croatoan, the stated destination of the colony.

Did we even have a rapier though, or was it just a door hinge? If it was a rapier, could it have been a seventeenth-century one? The only way to know for sure was to get the rust off. You cannot just scrub the rust off because it will probably break the artifact or risk damage to it. The process is a very slow one called electrolysis. We had already done electrolysis to an eleven-inch gun barrel and the now famous firebar that was probably used by the first English forge in America. For this mystery iron, the process was more difficult.

In electrolysis the artifact is hooked up to a negative electric current while a perfectly good piece of pure iron is hooked up to a positive current. (Think about jumping a car battery.) Both iron objects are submerged in clean water that has a special solution mixed in it to increase conductivity. Hydrogen gas is produced, and the natural process of rust is reversed. The rust leaves the artifact and binds to the positively charged object. This only works with what is called red rust. There are other types of rust—black and yellow—that require different methods of removal. Most of the rust on our artifacts is red rust and therefore fairly easily removed. It is a slow process; one nail can take eight hours of electrolysis.

The problem with the mystery object was that this process only works on the side of the artifact in direct line of sight of the modern iron. The shape of the artifact had several curves, and therefore, the object had to be turned many times and the process repeated. Doing a single side takes half a day.

After three days and nights of electrolysis, the mystery object was ready for a wipe down. The last bit of rust comes off like mud; you simply run water over it. The key to this rapier-shaped iron being a rapier would be if a hole went through the center of the thick part, indicating where the blade connected to the handle. The part we had was hopefully the decorative crossbar of a swept hilt rapier. I was the lucky one who got to rinse it off. When I could see my thumb on the other side, I did a double take. I was looking through the hole we hoped would be there. Even though I thought it was part of a rapier, this conformation was a happy surprise. It also had a silver heart with a cross under the heart in the dead center of the crossbar. This could be a maker's mark, but so far, we haven't been able to find the maker, as hearts and crosses were quite common.

I called Dr. Horton from the lab to tell him the good news but got no answer, as he was busy making another discovery on site. The rapier now had to be dipped in acetone, dried and then sealed in a special wax and preserved, so I snapped a few photos and sent them to Dr. Horton before the wax went on so you could see the heart and cross better. He rang back and said to come to the site, as he had found something even better. He wouldn't tell me on the phone, and I couldn't imagine what it could be.

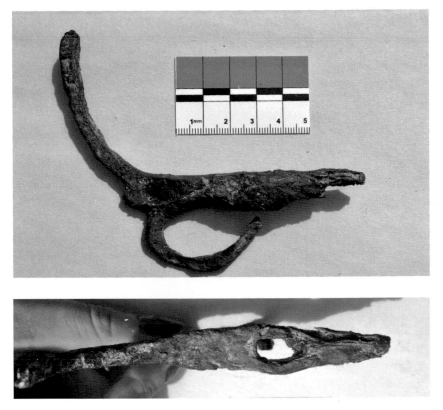

Top: Sixteenth-century swept hilt rapier. *Author's collection.*

Bottom: Top view of the sixteenth-century swept hilt rapier. *Author's collection.*

What he found was an item I had not even thought of before. It was two pieces of a writing slate that had faint drawings on them. The slate would later be examined by NASA. As a cherry on top, a lead pencil was found as well a few inches away from the slate. Could this day get any better? Yes. As darkness approached, one of if not the coolest artifact we have found emerged. Earlier in this book, you read about a gun barrel that was repurposed to tap trees for sap. The repurposing of English goods to fit Native needs is always a neat discovery. We found the ultimate repurposed tool: a glass arrowhead. The Croatoan had no glass, so the glass came from the English, but it was made into an arrowhead. This arrowhead was featured in the June 2018 *National Geographic* magazine along with our rapier and some other artifacts. We were starting to get little pieces of the colony.

Clockwise from top left: Glass arrowhead, sixteenth century. *Author's collection*; Sixteenth-century lead pencil. *Photo by Dr. Mark Horton*; Sixteenth-century hook-and-eye closure. *Photo by Dr. Mark Horton*; Double-heart leather fitting. *Photo by Dr. Mark Horton*; Writing slate, sixteenth century. *Photo by Dr. Mark Horton.*

A writing slate is not the sort of thing that would be traded to the Croatoan because they did not write. The colony was able to get all they needed from the Croatoan with simple scraps of copper, glass beads and other trinkets. There was no need to trade anything of actual value. The writing slate and pencil are from the sixteenth century. The biggest piece came from the top center of the slate. The slate was analyzed by NASA because of a faint drawing of a man shooting a gun that could be seen with a magnifying glass. Closer examination had too many overlapping drawings and scratches to hold anything firm.

A few other sixteenth-century artifacts emerged, including a hook-and-eye closure. Clothing, however, was often handed down, so it is possible the hook and eye arrived in the seventeenth century but equally likely it came in the sixteenth century.

One of the more interesting finds that puzzled the grad students and volunteers who dug it up was a double-heart leather fitting. Of course, Dr. Horton knew exactly what it was immediately.

Chapter 16

SURVIVORS' CAMP

The press began to take notice of what we were discovering. The Travel Channel contacted Dr. Horton and asked if it could include our dig in an episode of *Expedition Unknown*. Dr. Horton was off digging in Africa and told representatives to contact the Croatoan Archaeological Society. They wanted us to conduct a dig for them. The Travel Channel ended up flying over two of the archaeologists from England, Rosie Ireland and Charlie Gouge. They had been working under Dr. Horton on this project for years. Rosie and Charlie, together with myself and CAS board member Janet Bigney, were instructed by Dr. Horton to dig a trench for the show but to stop once we got to the 1650 glass bead level. Although both of these archaeologists were and are capable and professional, it was decided to go no deeper than the 1650s without Dr. Horton and to only do a small pit. The artifacts we had found previously were what the show really wanted to see, and we merely needed to demonstrate the process of digging and sifting. A true dig cannot be done properly by four people in two days.

The hole we dug was no bigger than the size of a boogie board, yet we found glass trade beads from Venice, Italy, along with Croatoan pottery, a few pipes and loads of turtle bones. They looked at the rapier and a few other key items that were brought to the site from the display room. The next television network to contact us was Discovery Science Channel. This time, thankfully, Dr. Horton would be available and could answer all of the tough questions.

Dr. Horton had been thinking about the Nuremberg tokens. One had been found on Hatteras Island in the 1930s, three had been found on Roanoke Island in the 1950s and then we had found another one on Hatteras Island in 2013. The ones from Roanoke had been in storage, and ours was on display in Hatteras Village. Today, Roanoke has finally put theirs on display, but the one that was given to them from Hatteras in the '30s they oddly put in storage in Florida, and apparently they can't find it. It was this first token that had Mark thinking.

Everything we had found had come from Croatoan village sites. Those sites were well known because they continued to exist into the 1700s and no one ever didn't know where they were. They were a great place to start a dig because at the very least one would learn more about the Natives. While it seems obvious that the 1587 colony—or rather, some of their stuff—would end up in the hands of their hosts, no one had ever located the survivors' camp. The colony did not know they were abandoned. They would have set up their own houses and camp somewhere. Dr. Horton wanted to know exactly where the first token had been found. The man who found the first token, Tandy, was my fourth-grade teacher's father. He had also told archaeologist William Haag where he had found the token, and Haag recorded the latitude. We discovered this when moving a bookshelf at the Hatteras Library and found a copy of the Haag report under the shelf.

I took Dr. Horton to the site of the first token. When we got there, Dr. Horton explained why it would have been the perfect spot on the island for a survivors' camp due to the unique geography that would have benefited the colony. Unlike our token, this one had been found about as far away from the Indian villages as you can get and still be on the island. So how did it get there? It was worth a look.

With cameras from Discovery Channel rolling, Dr. Horton used a special type of drone that can see different levels of chlorophyll and all sorts of other features to fly over the site. I thought it was kind of risky because we might find nothing, and Discovery would leave with nothing new. They did not want to show what had already been seen on Travel Channel, and *National Geographic* was at our dig site doing stuff for their magazine article, which created an unspoken tension. My idea was to show them a different Croatoan village site. I am glad no one listened to me.

Dr. Horton ended up discovering what appears to be a fort right where that token was found. He launched the drone and flew it back and forth to canvass a large area in the pattern of a rectangle. The images the drone took were then loaded into a computer. The different levels of chlorophyll and elevation were displayed on the screen in colors that ranged from red to yellow to green. There, in an open field surrounded by high wooded ground on three sides and the sea on the other, was a perfect rectangular object. We took measurements after seeing it on the computer screen and wondered how we did not see it from a hilltop before. It was a perfect rectangle with a north–south orientation. The Discovery episode showed us finding a fort but never explained the significance of the token or why we chose to look in that spot in the first place. This fort is the future of our project.

This was actually the second fort I helped find; the first was on Roanoke Island. Back in 2007, I was doing research for a Civil War talk and found Union soldiers who wrote about camping at the site of the 1585 fort, which has never been located. These soldiers said that the day after visiting the earthworks of the 1585 fort, they traveled north and found the abandoned guns of the Second North Carolina, a regiment of Confederate troops that ditched their guns into a creek before surrendering. I knew exactly which creek they were talking about, so I hiked out there and headed south. I found an odd ditch.

I told the newspaper *Outer Banks Sentinel*, and it ran a story. Later, I helped survey the area and map out the trench with Dr. Horton. It traveled in an odd shape but did loop around to form a full enclosure. It is shaped like an elongated Mickey Mouse symbol with two round-looking ears like the bastions found at the Jamestown Fort. We nicknamed it Fort Blob. The circumference was measured with a kite string by myself and historical interpreter Warren McMaster at 580 feet. The National Park Service looked at this fort and said it did not know what it was.

Apparently, a coin from the 1560s was found by a local man nearby. It is called the Adler Creek site. When I showed it to the NPS, they admitted it looked man-made. They didn't know what it was yet did absolutely nothing about it. It is on NPS land, so perhaps one day they will look into it.

The fort Dr. Horton found on Hatteras is on private land, so we will investigate it with property owner permission to see if it is the survivors' camp of the colony. Ralph Lane's fort (the one built on Roanoke in 1585) is clearly indicated as being on the northwest side of Roanoke, as discussed earlier. The representation of Fort Raleigh located on the east side of Roanoke was built in the 1950s. It is not authentic, but it is where they found their Nuremberg tokens and undoubtedly a prime spot for archaeology. Unfortunately, the parking lot for the *Lost Colony* play covers almost the entire area, so the digs that have taken place there have been limited to what has not been covered in asphalt.

Hopefully, we can find the survivors' camp next. Finding English goods in the Croatoan villages makes sense and is pretty good evidence that the colony assimilated there. Finding the survivors' camp would solve the mystery of where the colony went once and for all.

Chapter 17

THEORIES

The model for colonization that Raleigh, Harriot, White and Hakluyt envisioned of harmony with the Native peoples and mutually benefiting societies almost happened, even if only on a tiny island called Croatoan. Unfortunately, this model for settlement was abandoned just like the 1587 colony.

To this day, you cannot find a more complete ethnography of tidewater Indians than the one Thomas Harriot made in the late sixteenth century. The English did not attempt to understand Native society again until the eighteenth century, when John Lawson was commissioned to study tribes in North Carolina. Lawson, shockingly, is the next surviving record of Hatteras Island. The entire 1600s is missing from the written word. As mentioned earlier, the next time someone finally went to Croatoan after John White was not for one hundred years; John Lawson visited Hatteras and was told by the tribe they were descendants of white people who came on Raleigh's ship and that their ancestors could speak out of a book. What Lawson learned about the culture of the tribes he visited is also very telling. Lawson boldly wrote:

> *They naturally posses the righteous man's gift; they are patient under all afflictions and have a great many other natural vertues, which I have touched throughout the account of these savages. They are really better to us, than we are to them; they always give us victuals at their quarters, and take care we are armed against hungar and thirst: We look upon them with scorn and disitain and think them little better than beasts in human*

shape, though if well examined, we shall find that for all our religion and education, we posess more moral deformities and evils than these savages do or are aquainted withal.

After Lawson, there is very little reference to the Hatteras/Croatoan tribe. They fought on the side of the English in the Tuscarora War (1711–15) and apparently appealed to the Governor's Council for "Some Small relief from ye Country for their services being reduced to great poverty." A mere sixteen bushels of corn were issued to the Hatteras tribe from the public store by the Governor's Council for their help in defeating the Tuscarora. The Tuscarora had attacked English settlements along the Pamlico and Neuse Rivers in 1711. These attacks wiped out entire towns and even mutilated some of the victims. Lawson himself was burned to death by the Tuscarora. An interesting side note is that the pirate Blackbeard's sister was among the survivors of one such attack in Bath, North Carolina, that left three hundred English dead.

The last scrap of information on the Hatteras tribe comes from Governor Burrington in 1731. At that time, the tribe was still on the island but was reduced to fewer than twenty families. In other words, the Tuscarora War nearly wiped out what little was left of the tribe in the eighteenth century. A Hatteras Indian village also appears in the Buxton vicinity on a 1733 map called the Mosely map. By 1761, missionaries found a few people from the Hatteras and Roanoke tribes living together with remnants of other tribes by Lake Mattamuskeet, and that is the last mention of them in history. To be sure, a good number of them had assimilated with white settlers on the island, and over time, their genetics were simply overwhelmed by Caucasians. The land grant to the Hatteras tribe from Governor Dobbs is dated 1759 and lists European last names for the heads of households of the tribe. The grant was for two hundred acres on the sound side of Buxton on Hatteras Island.

∞

The Elizabethan voyages to the New World are a story of what could have been, almost was and, if not for a storm in 1590, might have been. When I stand on the beach at Hatteras Island and look out to the sea, as the colonists must have done, waiting for ships that never came, I can't help but wonder…what if?

I often think about the Natives during the contact period with the English, particularly Manteo. What a strange fate he had. I am sure as a boy he never could have imagined his future. Manteo met the first English explorers in 1584 and sailed back with them to England. He spent two months living on an English ship crossing the Atlantic Ocean and had to wonder when they would arrive. He and Wanchese were the first Americans ever to go to England, and while there, they met Queen Elizabeth. On the return voyage, he saw European warfare as the English unloaded cannons against Spanish ships and sacked Puerto Rico. Manteo was there when the Mandoag ambushed Ralph Lane in 1585 on the Chowan River. He was present when Lane ambushed and killed Wingina, the chief of the Secotan tribe. Manteo made another trip to England with none other than Francis Drake, probably England's most accomplished sea captain. Manteo was there for the birth of Virginia Dare, the first English child born on American soil. Manteo himself was the first American Indian baptized by the English. He was dubbed Lord of Roanoke and Dasamonquepeu by the English and left with the abandoned colony of 1587, who indicated they went to live in Manteo's hometown of Croatoan. It is logical that Manteo rests beneath the sands of Hatteras Island today. He deserves a plaque or statue or some sort of recognition other than the fictional role he has been tied to from the *Lost Colony* play. Almost all who have heard of him think he was a chief from Roanoke Island who fought against Wanchese, none of which is true.

∞

It has often been asked why no one from the abandoned colony contacted Jamestown a mere twenty years later. The colony would almost certainly have gotten word about the English return to the New World at some point. The assumption is that they had all died already.

Most people are not aware that the winter of 1600–1 was one of the harshest on record. A volcano called Huaynaputina erupted in Peru on February 19, 1600, spitting a lot of ash into the sky. It is comparable to the 1883 eruption of Krakatoa and is estimated to be one of the largest eruptions on Earth in the last two thousand years. Huaynaputina caused a horrifically cold winter that killed thousands across Russia and Europe.

The oral history of the Native Americans in North Carolina given to John Lawson in 1701 was that one hundred years prior (1601), the Neuse River froze so solid it could be walked across at the width of a mile and that many people perished. This date fits with the global bad winter of the northern hemisphere caused by the volcano. For those not familiar with North Carolina, the Neuse River does not freeze over. In fact, on the coast it is considered a lot if it snows more than two inches a year. If the oral history is even remotely true, it means the Pamlico Sound would also have frozen. The Pamlico freezing for any length of time would devastate the Croatoan.

In the winter that followed the eruption, wine production in France was destroyed, and the effects are mentioned worldwide. Was the winter of 1601 the straw that broke the camel's back for the colony? If so, why did the tribe survive and not the colony? Could this winter have frozen the Pamlico Sound and caused the colony to divide? Who knows?

Another theory that many have put forth is that after some time, the colony left Croatoan and headed to Chesapeake, where they were later killed by Powhatan Indians. This idea has some weak support from the primary sources. Chesapeake Bay was where the colony was supposed to go in 1587 before the ship's pilot, Simon Fernando (a former Portuguese pirate), refused to take them there. It is reasonable speculation that the colonists might have thought John White never made it back to England and that the resupply ships were headed to Chesapeake, and thus the colonists, or some of them at least, headed up there to check.

Powhatan told John Smith of a few white people living with the Chesapeake Indians whom he had killed before or shortly after the Jamestown settlers arrived. These white men may also have been the remnants of the thirteen men chased off by the Secotan in 1586. There is a brief mention of the Chesapeake Indians by Ralph Lane in 1585. Lane stated that he had two Chesapeake Indians with him when he ambushed Wingina, so some contact with this tribe must have transpired prior to the 1587 colony's arrival.

However, the source for Powhatan telling John Smith about some white people living with the Chesapeake Indians does not come from John Smith. In fact, Smith never mentions anything in his accounts that even hints white people were living with the Chesapeake Indians or of any slaughter of this tribe by Powhatan. This idea was put forth instead by English cleric Samuel Purchase in 1625 in an anti-Indian propaganda piece titled "Virginia's Verger." Purchase claims that Smith told him of this dubious tale, yet Smith, who gives two of the most detailed accounts of early Jamestown, never mentioned it in his own accounts. It is important to consider the historical context to understand the mindset of Purchase when (clearly) he made up this information. The Powhatan in 1622 had slaughtered over three hundred Jamestown colonists, including women and children, after hiding hatchets under furs they were pretending to bring into the fort to trade. When Purchase made up this tale pinning the murder of the Lost Colony on the Powhatan, it was during the height of conflict with that tribe, and Powhatan was already dead and thus could not dispute it.

Spanish accounts tell us that in June 1588, not quite a year after the "Lost" Colony was abandoned, they searched the Chesapeake Bay thoroughly and found no trace of or even word of the English colony.

It is also possible that the colony—or again some of them—made a break for home and were lost at sea. Contrary to popular fiction that states the colonists were left with no boats, they had two pinnaces, which are small ships up to forty feet in length. We know that a pinnace was built and sailed from Puerto Rico to the Outer Banks in 1585 with Richard Grenville and Thomas Cabindish, who captained the *Tiger* and the *Elizabeth*, respectively. Therefore, it was possible for a small ship to cross the ocean, although not recommended. If the colony went to Croatoan only to later try and sail home, it would explain why no one from the colony ever contacted Jamestown, which was settled a mere twenty years later.

Another theory that is somewhat alluded to in the Jamestown records is that the colony was at some point enslaved by Indians to mine copper. The abandoned colony did include some Welsh miners, and copper was valued by the Natives as much as gold was by Europeans. Probably the most useful skill the colonists would have had to offer the Natives would have been mining and metal working. The smelted copper bun found on Hatteras Island in the same context as the Nuremberg token had a small sample of shavings tested. The presence of large levels of arsenic and a good look at the isotopes tell us if the copper is in fact European. This test was explained on the History Channel's *In Search Of*, hosted by Zachary Quinto in 2019, and featured the copper bun we excavated and tested in 2015.

It is possible that the colonists were mining copper and bringing it back to Croatoan to be worked. In the first year, the colony would not have had any way of knowing they had been abandoned and might have been searching for silver and other precious metals to make a huge profit from once the English returned. They also could have simply been after copper, which would allow them to contribute something to their host tribe.

In the spring of 1608, the chief of the Paspahegh in eastern Virginia told William Strachey that the colonists were at a place called "Panawicke beyond Roonok" and offered to take them there, although this never came to fruition, according to Rountree. Roonok was probably Roanoke Island, and beyond it was a place called Paquiwoc, modern-day Avon on Hatteras Island.

Unknown copper item. *Author's collection.*

There was also a town that looks to be near Chocowinity, North Carolina, called Panauuioc, but there is no connection to that town or mention of it in the primary sources. It was also located in the heart of enemy territory.

If what John Smith heard in 1607 about the colony being at a "great turing of saltwater" and what Strachey was told about them hunting for copper were both true, it may be that some were mining copper and bringing it back to the island. As it stands now, there simply is not enough evidence to come to any solid conclusions. What is puzzling is that no attempt was made by Jamestown to go to the coast to Croatoan or to the mountains to seek out the colonists. The reason for the lack of motivation to find a twenty-year-old colony is probably because Jamestown had its hands full just surviving. Perhaps after 154 of 214 died in one year, Jamestown assumed the colony from twenty years back was as good as dead, and they may have been correct. The only expeditions to search for the colony were halfhearted trips to Chowan in North Carolina and to Nottoway lands near the coast of Virginia. These odd adventures to lands not even remotely close to where the colonists had reportedly been seen turned up absolutely nothing other than proving they were not in the Chowan Indian village (modern-day Bertie County) nor in Nottoway. King James had motivation not to find the colony because if found, it would strengthen the claims and hold on lands by Sir Walter Raleigh and the other investors whom the king hated. Eventually, King James had Raleigh and most of the queen's inner circle arrested, killed or both, including Raleigh.

How did all the sixteenth-century English artifacts end up in Croatoan? Perhaps it is all from the 1585 voyage and not 1587. This is unlikely given the presence of mixed architecture found at the site. Square beam building among dozens of longhouses indicated the Lost Colony because the men in 1585 slept in military field tents on Croatoan. The forge is also an indication of 1587. The 1585 group was only on the island for a couple months and with only twenty people to spot ships, not to build a town and set up a forge.

There are more questions than answers. We still don't know exactly how much of Hatteras Island has been lost to erosion in the last 430 years, or, for that matter, Roanoke Island as well. Both islands have tree stumps jutting out of the water and obvious signs of land loss, but exactly how much is anyone's guess. The motherload of artifacts may very well be under water or destroyed long ago by development. Tales of dozens of skeletons being found when houses were built 30 and 40 years ago are common. The Croatoan site is littered with modern houses, septic fields and driveways. It is amazing we have been able to locate any archaeology undisturbed and intact.

Another interesting account to consider when it comes to the smelted copper we found in the Croatoan village site comes from one of the most unlucky men in the sixteenth century, Darby Glande. Glande was an Irishman pressed into service twice by the English. He was part of Grenville's 1585 voyage. He returned again in the 1587 voyage, presumably pressed into service for a second time. Darby escaped the English on the way over in 1587 at Puerto Rico, finally ending his servitude. This freedom was short-lived, however, because he was almost instantly captured by the Spanish and sent to prison for seven years of hard labor.

During his capture, Glande was interrogated by the Spanish. He told the Spanish that Richard Grenville had taken an arroba (twenty-five pounds) of native copper back to England in 1585 to be tested for any silver mixed in. Glande also reported to the Spanish that he once had a pearl the size of an acorn, which was given to him by the Natives of Croatoan, but this pearl had been confiscated from him by Grenville once he found out about it.

Glande was very helpful to the Spanish, providing details on the number of ships and men the English had, and he even gave the latitude of the inlet the English had entered. Interestingly, that latitude matched the latitude given by Governor John White for the northeast corner of Croatoan: 35.5 degrees. One must keep in mind that for the first few months of the 1585 voyage and for the entirety of the 1584 voyage, the base of operations was not Roanoke Island but Croatoan. Grenville was only in the New World from June until August 25, 1585, and supplies and men were not transferred to Roanoke until August 24. This means that Grenville either spent only one day on Roanoke Island in 1585 or perhaps not at all. Therefore, if Grenville was interested in testing Native copper, as Glande reported to the Spanish that he was, then the first tests performed (for the purpose of seeing what other elements such as silver could be separated from the copper) would have taken place on Croatoan.

German metallurgist Joachim Ganz accompanied the 1585 English voyage specifically to test metals found in the New World. This German is the most likely one to have tokens from Nuremberg, and our token was found near a smelted copper bun and iron firebar and ceramics from a sixteenth-century Germanic jug. As an interesting side note, Ganz was the first Jewish person to come to America.

Could it be we have found artifacts from both 1585 and 1587? More investigation may answer this question. For every question that was answered, it seemed two more emerged. No doubt the fort Dr. Horton has located thanks to a token found in the 1930s and modern technology is the future of the project. Science is an endless quest for knowledge, and history is a puzzle that can never be fully completed. I believe our digs have uncovered a wealth of information and added a little more to the mystery of the abandoned colony. It is my hope that the Croatoan will not be forgotten and that their true role in history will one day be taught in schools. May they live on in our minds and hearts, for if so, they are truly eternal. Their art and tools and housewares are on display for all to see in Hatteras Village, and it costs nothing to view them. Preserving the history of the Croatoan has always been the goal of the Croatoan Archaeological Society, and I encourage all to learn more.

ALGONQUIAN GLOSSARY

Croatoan comes from the Algonquian word *kurawoten* (kuh-ra-woe-tain) and means "council town." It is the original name of Hatteras Island. Algonquian is not a tribe or a language but a language family with at least twenty-nine dialects. The following is a list of words used by the Croatoan. The language is sometimes referred to as Carolina Algonquian and was also spoken by the Pamlico, Chowan and Currituck Indians, among others. The following list is from the Coastal Carolina Indian Center.

apis: sit down
ar-rounser: shot (lead shot)
artamockes: bluejay (bird)
asanamawqueo: loon (bird)
ascopo: sweet bay (tree)
chachaquises: woodpecker (bird)
chaham: shad (fish)
chicamacomico: place that is swept
chingwusso: channel bass (fish)
chuwon: paint
coppatuseo: sturgeon (fish)
coscushaw: greenbrier root (used to make bread)
cosh: ten
crenepos: women
croatoan: council town or permanent town

dasamonquepeu: peninsula
ehqutonahas: stop talking (shut up)
guapacina: brass
gun tock seik: gunlock
hinds: flint
ka ka torwawirocs yowo: how is this called?
keetrauk: catfish
Kew'as: idol of accessorial god
kewasowock: idols
kinnakeet: land jutting out sharply
kowabetteo: garfish
kupi: yes
kurustuwes nir: listen to me
kuwumaras: I love you
maachone: belt
machicomuc: temple
macocqwer: melon or gourd
mahta: no
mamankanois: butterfly
manchauemec: croaker (fish)
mangummenauk: acorn of live oak
manteo: to snatch
masunnehockeo: sheepshead (fish)
mattosh: blanket
meeaquous: cardinal (bird)
memelkson: skink
menatonan: he who listens well
metequesunnak: cactus bulb
mincon: food
minsal: beads of necklace
mishcosk: red
mis-kis-su: necklace
moc-cose: needle or awl
Monto'ac: Great Spirit or God
mottau-quahan: hat
mowcottowosh: black
mushaniq: squirrel
nau-haush-shoo: eight
nek: my mother

neshinnauh: two
nesh-wonner: three
nipatas: stand up
nohsh: my father
numohshomus: my grandfather
nunohum: my grandmother
nuntanuhs: my daughter
Nuppin: Indians
nuqisus: my son
nuturuwins: I am called
okindgier: beans
oonossa: pine tree
opossum: to carry in a pouch
pach-ic-conk: nine
pagatowr: corn
paquiwoc: people of the shallow water
perquimans: place where beautiful women are found
popogusso: Hell
pumitukew: river (also where the word *Pamlico* comes from)
pungue: gunpowder
pyas: come here!
rakiock: cypress (tree)
rapputoc: a flap
reapoke: devil
rig-cosq: knife
rosh-shocquon: hoe
sacquenuckot: skunk
sacquenummener: yaupon berry
sa kir winkan?: Are you well?
sapummener: chestnut
secotan: burning ground
seekanauk: horseshoe crab
tama-bick: axe
tapisco: gold
taus-won: coat
tesicqueo: king snake
teteszo: striped bass (fish)
tinda: fire
top-po-osh: seven

tosh-shonte: Englishman
umpe (nupuy): water
umperren: five
untoc: four
uppowoc: tobacco or to smoke
waboose: bunny, baby rabbit
wanchese: to take flight from water
wassador: metal
weembot: one
weesacoon: rum
who-yeoc: six
wickonzowr: peas
winauk: sassafras
win-gan-a-coa: welcome friend (when talking to a stranger)
wingapo: how are you/hello
winkan Nupes: sleep well
wiroans: leader, councilman
wop-poshaumosh: white (color)
wutapantam: deer
yapam: ocean
yau-ooner: four
yehawkans: house

This dictionary can be found on the Coastal Carolina Indian Center website at www.coastalcarolinaindians.com.

BIBLIOGRAPHY

Barlowe, Arthur. *The First Voyage to Roanoke*. 1584. Repr., Chapel Hill: University of North Carolina, n.d. docsouth.unc.edu/nc/barlowe/barlowe.html.

The Barnes Review: A Journal of Natural Thought and History 119, no. 3 (May–June 2013).

Coastal Carolina Indian Center. www.coastalcarolindiancenter.com.

Griffin, Nigel. *A Short Account of the Destruction of the Indies*. New York: Penguin, 1992.

Harrington, Jean C. *Search for the Cittie of Raleigh: Archaeological Excavations at Fort Raleigh National Historic Site*. Washington, D.C.: National Park Service, U.S. Department of Interior, 1962.

Harriot, Thomas. *A Briefe and True Report of the New Found Land of Virginia: The Complete 1590 Theodor de Bry Edition*. New York: Dover Publications, 1972.

Hatteras Monitor 14, no. 8 (1999): 11.

Lane, Ralph. *Raleigh's First Roanoke Colony*. Repr., Chapel Hill: University of North Carolina, n.d. docsouth.unc.edu/nc/lane/lane.html.

Lawson, John. *A New Voyage to Carolina*. 1709. Repr., Whitefish, MT: Kessinger Publishing, 2004.

Lorant, Stefan. *The New World: The First Pictures of America*. New York: Beck Engraving Inc., 1946.

MacNeill, Ben D. *The Hatterasman*. Wilmington: Publishing Laboratory, University of North Carolina, 2008.

Mathis, Mark A., and Jeffery J. Crow. *The Prehistory of North Carolina: An Archaeological Symposium*. Raleigh: North Carolina Department of Cultural Resources Division of Archives and History, 1983.

Perkins, Sid. "Disaster Goes Global: The Eruption in 1600 of a Seemingly Quiet Volcano in Peru Changed Global Climate and Triggered Famine as Far Away as Russia." *Science News* 174, no. 5 (2008): 16–21.

Phelps, David. *Guide to the Croatan Archaeological Site Collection*. (#1061). Special Collections Department, J.Y. Library, East Carolina University, Greenville, North Carolina.

Powell, William S. *North Carolina through Four Centuries*. Chapel Hill: University of North Carolina Press, 1989.

Purdue, Theda. *Native Carolinians: The Indians of North Carolina*. Raleigh: North Carolina Department of Cultural Resources Division of Archives and History, 1985.

Quinn, David Beers. *A New World*. New York: Berkley Trade Publishing, 1995.

———. *The Roanoke Voyages, 1585–1590*. Ser. 2, vol. 104. Cambridge, UK: Hakluyt Society, n.d.

Rountree, Helen C. *Pocahontas's People: The Powhatan Indians of Virginia through Four Centuries*. Norman: University of Oklahoma Press, 1990.

———. *Powhatan Indians of Virginia*. N.p., n.d.

Ward, H. Trawick, and R.P. Stephen Davis. *Time Before History: The Archaeology of North Carolina*. Chapel Hill: University of Chapel Hill Press, 1999.

INDEX

ABOUT THE AUTHOR

Scott Dawson is a native of Hatteras Island whose family roots on the island trace back to the 1600s. He is a well-known local historian, author and amateur archaeologist. He is president and founder of the Croatoan Archaeological Society and has participated in a decade of archaeological excavations and research on Hatteras Island under the direction of Dr. Mark Horton. He also serves on the board of directors of the Outer Banks History Center. He is a graduate of the University of Tennessee with a BA in psychology and minor in history. He lives with his wife, Maggie, and two daughters, Kirra and Sabra, on the Outer Banks of North Carolina. He is an avid surfer and loves all things outdoors. He is active in his community as a volunteer firefighter, EMT, teacher at College of the Albemarle, youth soccer coach and historical public speaker.

Visit us at
www.historypress.com